Rethinking our world
Second edition

Philip Higgs
Jane Smith

Rethinking our world: *Second edition*

First edition 2000
Second edition 2006
Reprinted 2007
Reprinted 2008
by Juta & Co.
Mercury Crescent
Wetton, 7780
Cape Town, South Africa

© 2006 Juta & Co. Ltd

ISBN-13: 978-0-70217-255-7

All rights reserved. No part of this publication may be reproduced or transmitted in any form or by any means, electronic or mechanical, including photocopying, recording, or any information storage or retrieval system, without permission in writing from the publisher.

Typeset in 10.5 pt on 14pt Adelon Light

Project manager: Sarah O'Neill
Editor: Sandy Shepherd
Indexer: Cecily van Gend
Illustrator: Bronwen Lusted
DTP and design: Charlene Bate
Cover designer: WaterBerry Designs cc
Printed in South Africa by Creda Communications, Epping.

The authors and the publisher have made every effort to obtain permission for and to acknowledge the use of copyright material. Should any infringement of copyright have occurred, please contact the publisher, and every effort will be made to rectify omissions or errors in the event of a reprint or new edition.

Contents

Introduction v

1 Thinking clearly and learning from experience:
  the beginning of our new world 1

2 Asking questions: challenging what the world tells us 17

3 How in the world can we give our lives meaning? 32

4 What of an African world? 43

5 Can we change our world? 61

6 Rethinking a woman's world 88

7 Who in the world am I? 103

8 Is there a world that speaks to us? 116

9 Where in the world are we going? 130

Conclusion 141

Bibliography 143

Acknowledgements 144

Recommended reading 145

Index 147

Introduction

When we showed a draft of this book to one of our friends, her comment was: "You're going to upset a lot of people with this book." But philosophy by its very nature, asks difficult and subversive questions.

Philosophy does not allow us to rest contently in life, nor does it allow us to "go with the flow", to accept passively what society tells us and wants us to believe.

Philosophy is averse to any form of mediocrity and compromise. It wants us to rethink, recreate, transform.

The world's revolutionaries have all been philosophers: Moses, Karl Marx, Jesus, Mohammed, Socrates, Mahatma Gandhi, Martin Luther King, Nelson Mandela.

The world's great thinkers have been philosophers: Plato, Augustine, Albert Einstein, Friedrich Nietzsche, Jacques Derrida.

The world's feminists have been philosophers: Mary Wollstonecraft, Liz Sanger, the Pankhursts, Germaine Greer, Mary Daly, Ama Ata Aidoo, Maria Nzomo, Neuma Aguiar.

Philosophy begins when human beings start questioning their world. We might as well admit that society, no matter where we live, does not encourage people to become philosophers and to question what is going on around them. Questioning and debate in our contemporary, globalised society has sunk to the level of TV chat shows and idiotic radio phone-ins. All we hear and get exposed to is mindless contradiction. Even the newspapers gloss over important, serious issues. The Internet is also proving to be a disappointment, although there are a few websites run by people who try to encourage critical and in-depth reasoning.

Philosophy is available to everybody. It does not give us a simple creed to follow or a message of comfort, but it has the power to emancipate us from destructive illusions. It also has the power to make us creators of new worlds. In the pages that follow we invite you to participate in the process of rethinking our world.

one — Thinking clearly and learning from experience: the beginning of our new world

What did you do today? What did you do yesterday?
What do you plan to do tomorrow?
Next week?
Next month?
How long do you think you've got to live?
Do you know anyone who is dying?
Are you looking forward to tomorrow? Do you hope it's going to be better than yesterday? Or was today fine for you?

Wanting to have a better tomorrow has caused a lot of people to do many things: change their job, get divorced, have another child, get rid of the government, start wars, end wars, write peace treaties, form new governments.

The following is a quotation from a document written by a group of men and women who wanted a better tomorrow:

> We, the people of South Africa,
> Recognise the injustices of the past;
> Honour those who suffered for justice and freedom in our land;
> Respect those who have worked to build and develop our country; and
> Believe that South Africa belongs to all who live in it, united in our diversity.
> We therefore, through our freely elected representatives, adopt this
> Constitution as the supreme law of the Republic so as to –
> Heal the divisions of the past and establish a society based on democratic
> Values, social justice and fundamental human rights ….
> May God protect our people.

This document was written recently, in 1996. It is the Constitution of the Republic of South Africa.

Read through the excerpt again and underline the words you feel are the most important in this context.

Rethinking our world

Question > What words did you underline?

_____

_____

Our response
We thought the following words were the most important:
justice; freedom; democratic values; fundamental human rights, God
  Your list is probably similar to ours. Of all the words above, which do you think is the most important? _____

Of all the words in the excerpt from the Constitution, we thought the most important was "freedom". But what do we mean by "freedom"? This is not an easy question to answer, but it is the sort of critical, difficult question that philosophy encourages us to ask. It is the sort of question that helps us to start thinking clearly.

The following paragraph, "Just supposing ...", is part of our answer to the question: What is freedom?

Just supposing ...

Just supposing there was a planet not for from Earth called Happyplace. On this planet, everyone has enough food to eat, nice clothes to wear, nice homes to live in and nobody ever feels hatred, anger, fear, pain or jealousy. On Happyplace, everyone gets along fine with each other and everyone does jobs they like. It sounds great, and we decide to get on a spaceship and go there to get away from all our problems. Before the people who run Happyplace agree to us staying, however, they tell us that the reason everyone gets along with everyone else is that, on Happyplace, everyone has to take a pill every day, which stops them experiencing any negative emotions. The people who run Happyplace get together every morning to make sure they all take this pill. There's no need to worry, though: this pill is wonderful. It doesn't have any side-effects, we don't have to pay for it and, best of all, it ensures that we'll have a nice, peaceful life.

We would not be prepared to live on Happyplace, despite all its advantages. In fact, the thought of living somewhere where you are forced to take a drug every day to make sure you don't experience pain, sadness, anger or hate is, we believe, horrifying.

It sounds like the sort of mind control that extreme religious cults go in for. In fact, to us, it sounds like the worst sort of slavery.

So, in answer to the question "What is freedom?" we would start by saying:
- A free person is someone who is **not forced** to do something.
- Freedom involves the expression of the whole of human experience, including negative emotions such as pain, fear, etc.
- Freedom means not having someone else, or society, "messing with your head".

Of course, freedom means many other things too.

What do words mean?

Look at the word you wrote down as the most important from the excerpt and ask yourself "What does this word actually mean?" Use a dictionary if you need to, but try to give the word some real, concrete expression.

Perhaps you chose the words "human rights".

First of all, do you agree that this phrase is used often these days? We frequently hear the media talking about "human rights violation", "human rights groups", and saying "such-and-such is a basic human right".

Look at the first word in this phrase: human. What is a human? A human is, we think, a member of the species *Homo sapiens*, which means "thinking man". Humans are characterised by having minds. We believe that the mind is more than just the brain, although the mind necessarily involves the brain. But, to us, "mind" means the indefinable interconnection between:
- thinking
- all the emotions
- consciousness
- subconsciousness
- the five senses: sight, touch, hearing, smell, taste
- memory
- intuition/sixth sense.

Not everybody would agree with our statement that a human is a being with an indefinable mind. Perhaps you disagree, too. Perhaps you believe that it is the material, highly evolved brain that makes us human.

We think that being human is also about being connected to other humans, although we have problems with the glib way in which *ubuntu* is presented today. We think that to be human means to have the freedom to live somewhere between the extremes of excessive individualism (the mistake of Western culture) and excessive communality (the mistake of African culture). The extremes are not desirable: the first leads to aggression and competitiveness and the second leads to passivity and hopelessness.

Rethinking our world

Another way of answering the question "What does the word 'human' mean?" is to respond by saying what the human is not:
- not an animal
- not a divine being (eg an angel or an elf)
- not a machine
- not a plant
- not an object
- not a thing.

As you can see, trying to answer the question "What is a human?" is quite difficult.

Activity

In the space below, write down your own description of what a human is. If you disagree with our views, say so. Try to say why you disagree.

_____

_____

_____

Now look at the next word in the expression "human rights" – the word "rights". This expression is at the core of the new Constitution, so we all need to have some idea of what we mean when we use it.

When we went to a dictionary for a definition of this word, we found something very interesting: the English word "right" has an enormous number of meanings. This is significant, because a word that means many things can easily be distorted or misused.

The nearest definition the dictionary had for our purposes was:

Right: A legal, moral title or claim to the possession of property or authority, the enjoyment of certain privileges.

In other words, we could say that a "human right" means "something that a human being can claim as his or hers according to an accepted standard of morality".

Thinking clearly and learning from experience

Activity

Is your first language English? If not, write down the nearest equivalent your language has to the English word "right". Then describe what that word means in your language.

Here are some concrete examples of a "human right" as defined in the English language:
- the right to nondiscrimination at work and in the public sphere
- the right to vote
- the right to own property
- the right to privacy
- the right to a fair hearing in a court of law
- the right to wages in return for work
- the right to choose one's religious adherence
- the right not to have any religious adherence
- the right to one's political views.

Activity

What legal rights do all South Africans have today that they didn't under apartheid? Write your answer in the space below.

Question

What about "rights" that can't be legally enforced, such as "the right to a job", "the right to housing", "the right to proper medical treatment"?

_____

_____

What is the difference between a right that can't be enforced in law and a right that can be enforced in law?

_____

_____

Our response

We think the difference between these two types of rights is that a right that can be enforced is a legal right and a right that cannot be enforced is a moral right. A good example of a moral right that has never been enforced anywhere in the world is our right to be treated as humans and not objects or machines in the pursuit of political, economic or military goals.

Philosophy and language: why words are important

"What is the meaning of a word?" is a question that doesn't get asked very often and yet all of us, all the time, use words. We have conversations with each other, we talk on the phone, we go to lectures, listen to teachers, read newspapers. The mass media is full of opinions, views, ideas, news commentary, talk shows and phone-ins.

The meaning of words is important in philosophy. Even if we cannot define exactly what we mean by a word – and we often can't – we need to be as precise as we can. This includes consciously being aware that we may well be using words that can't be defined clearly. If we don't take the trouble to do this, we risk living in a language community (of whatever language) that eventually becomes meaningless. We think this is already happening in the English language community, in the worlds of advertising and the media.

> **Activity**
>
> The next time you see an advertisement, or listen to one on the radio, stop looking at or listening to it and then ask yourself: what did the advertiser actually say to me?
>
> In the space below, write down what you saw or heard and then try to explain its message.

Analysing statements is one of the major tasks of philosophy: it helps us to think clearly and precisely.

Thinking clearly and precisely is regarded as important because we cannot be free or have a democratic society if we have never learned to think clearly.

> **Philosophers at work**
>
> As far as we know, the first philosopher who challenged us to think clearly was Plato. Plato lived in Greece, from about 428 to 347 BC. In his book, *Republic*, Plato repeatedly asked questions such as "What is truth?", "What is goodness?", "What is justice?" He used ordinary, everyday examples to demonstrate to his students that we need to be absolutely clear about what such words mean. According to Plato, the moment we start thinking clearly and precisely, our lives and the world around us take on new meaning.

Hidden assumptions

Look at the excerpt we started with, from the South African Constitution. It contains the following words:

> May God protect our people.

What does this tell us about the people who wrote the Constitution? It tells us that these people believe in God and – and this is important – that they assume we believe in God too. In other words, the words of the South African Constitution contain a hidden assumption.

A hidden assumption is something we should watch out for in any message we receive, whether written or spoken. Hidden assumptions are dangerous and manipulative. Advertisements contain hidden assumptions and so does much media reporting.

We would like to point out to the writers of the Constitution that not everybody believes in a God who can "protect" human beings. Recently America was hit by the devastation of Hurricane Katrina. Some months previously, large parts of Asia suffered the devastation of a huge tidal wave. In both cases, large numbers of people were killed and both events were followed by outbreaks of disease, homelessness and starvation.

There are other problems with the word "God".

- People who use the word "God" are often very vague about what God is really like. They tend to use "feel-good" words to describe God, such as "love", "creator", "spiritual", "Father in Heaven". Also, different people describe God in different ways. Christians describe God using one set of words, Muslims use another set of words and Hindus say there are many gods.
- Nobody can show us God. If people say something like "It's cold outside today", we can check whether they're speaking the truth by opening the door and going outside. There are lots of examples of this. If I say, "John is getting married to Mary on Saturday", and it's the first you've heard of it, all you've got to do is contact John or Mary and see what they say. Even complicated facts can be checked. If a scientist working on the US space programme tells us on TV that there are simple forms of life on the planet Mars, we can read newspapers and scientific articles to check whether other scientists agree with him or her. Maybe the space programme even has photographs taken on Mars of plants and fungi on rocks.

The point is that we cannot see God with our eyes, hear God with our ears or touch God with our fingers. There are no photographs of God. We cannot check to see if God exists. We cannot experience God with our senses (sight, smell, touch, hearing, taste).

It is for these reasons that some philosophers, particularly British philosophers, have claimed that statements about God are meaningless.

Activity

What is your response to our comments about God? Do you agree or disagree? Why?

Just supposing ...

One day you hear on the radio that scientists have invented a spaceship that can take human beings to all parts of space, way beyond our own galaxy, the Milky Way. For the first time ever, if we want to, we can book trips on this spaceship and go all around the Universe. This sounds exciting and you book your ticket. The spaceship leaves and takes you all over the Universe. You see stars, black holes and huge clouds of swirling dust and planets. But you don't see God. You ask the spaceship commander about this and he says, "Yes, well, I travel all over the Universe every day, and I've never seen God. That's because He doesn't exist."

Question

What is your response to the spaceship commander's reply?

Our response

We'll be discussing God and religion generally in more detail in a later chapter. In recent years, a number of contemporary philosophers have rejected the view that statements about God and religion are meaningless. Among them is the American writer, Ken Wilber. African philosophy also tends to reject the view that statements about God are meaningless. It is interesting too to note that the British scientist, John Polkinghorne, resigned his chair in Mathematical Physics at Cambridge, in 1979, to become an Anglican priest.

Linguistic analysis

Look at the following set of statements:
- One and one equals two.
- A physical object cannot be round and triangular at the same time.
- Either it is raining or it is not raining.
- No bachelor is married.
- A woman is either pregnant or not pregnant.

All these statements **must be true**. We do not have to check whether they are true. Statements that must be true fall into two categories:
- Mathematical statements
- Statements that contain the word "is" or the words "is not".

Statements that must be true (or false) are said to be "true (or false) by definition".

Philosophers at work

The philosophy that concentrates on trying to find the exact meaning of words is known as linguistic analysis. Linguistic analysis was a movement in early 20th-century philosophy. It was based on the thinking of Ludwig Wittgenstein and Bertrand Russell. Linguistic analysis claims that almost all philosophical problems can be dispensed with once their underlying linguistic basis is exposed. In other words, linguistic analysis claims that if, no matter how hard we try to solve a problem, we fail, then we are dealing with a false problem or, more likely, we are dealing with a meaningless set of words.

The most popular exponents of linguistic analysis as a means of arriving at truth were two British philosophers, Bertrand Russell (1872-1970) and A J Ayer (1910-1989). In their work, Russell and Ayer focused on three things: logic, linguistic meaning and verifiable facts. They attempted to find out how and why we know a statement is true, false or meaningless. They also attempted to "get to the bottom of reality" by closely analysing how language worked and by closely analysing what a "fact" is. Another philosopher, Ludwig Wittgenstein, started out as a supporter of linguistic analysis but moved away from this position, largely as a result of his experiences in World War I.

Does it work?

What linguistic analysis can help us to do

1. Think more clearly.
2. Be precise in what we mean.
3. Spot hidden assumptions in arguments.
4. Be aware of manipulation and dishonesty in all forms of propoganda, including the mass media.

What linguistic analysis can't help us with

1. Moral problems.
2. Life choices.
3. Facing our own mortality.
4. Seeing the people we love suffer.
5. Our own suffering.

Thinking clearly and learning from experience

Quick summary

Linguistic analysis is concerned with the question: "What is the meaning of this word or sentence?" More precisely: what is the meaning of these symbols?

> **Activity**
>
> Virtually all of us have a problem in our life that upsets us and which we cannot seem to solve. What is the biggest problem in your life right now?
>
> Write this problem out as clearly as you can and make a point of being precise about what you mean.
>
> Now write down why this problem is upsetting you so much. Again, be as clear and precise as you can.
>
> You may find, after doing this, that you feel a bit better about this problem. If you do not, look at the words you've written. Are all these words clear, precise and "tight"?

Logical symbolism and argument

The philosophical movement that focused on linguistic analysis also focused on logic. The aim was to get to what we might call the "bare bones" of truth.

For example: the following **must be true.**
- All humans are mortal
- John is a human
- Therefore John is mortal

Logic formalises such deductions with rules precise enough to programme a computer to decide if an argument is valid.

The aim of logic, in philosophy, is to arrive at the basic structure of truth. This process is facilitated by representing objects and relationships symbolically.

To take the example above: we could use h for the set of humans, m for the set of mortal creatures and V for Vuyo.

We use the symbolic expression "$x \in y$" to say that: object x is a member of category y.

Thus we represent "Vuyo is a human" with "$j \in h$".

We use the "quantifier" λ to indicate that all objects satisfy some condition. For example: "All humans are mortal" can be written as:

$\lambda\ x\ x \in h \rightarrow x \in m$.

This reads that every x that has the property of being human must also have the property of being mortal.

Then we restate the syllogism as follows:

$\lambda\ x\ x \in h \rightarrow x \in m\ v \in h$ therefore $v \in m$

This reads that anything that is of the category x, where x is a human, h, is also of the category mortal, m. Vuyo, v is of the category x, which therefore means that Vuyo is mortal.

Any statement that is true or false by definition can be expressed in the form of symbolic logic.

What is a fact?

So far, we have concentrated on language and how we need to analyse the words and symbols that make up our language community. But we don't just live in the world of language or the world of logic. We also live in the world of facts. This is the world of our everyday experience, the world we see around us.

Examples of everyday statements of facts are:
- It is sunny today and rather hot.
- Mary came to work early today.
- Harry is taking an examination tomorrow – he wants to pass.
- Sipho lives in Mamelodi.

These facts can be checked directly. We feel the heat and see the glare of the sun. We can see Mary sitting in her office. We heard Harry tell John about wanting to pass the exam. We have visited Sipho at his house in Mamelodi.

We rely on our senses to tell us things (we feel the heat, see the glare, and hear Harry talking to John). We believe what our senses tell us and we believe that the people around us hear, see and feel the same things we do.

We use our senses to tell us facts. We do this so naturally that we are not even aware of doing it.

Thinking clearly and learning from experience

Think, for a moment, about the following questions:
- How do you know where you live?
- How do you know what's for supper?
- How do you know what your spouse or friend looks like?
- How do you know, right now, that you're reading this book?

In everyday life, we use our senses and our experience to establish facts, to check facts. This is the most reliable form of knowledge and information we have.

Quick summary

The method of inquiry in philosophy that argues that experience gained through the traditional five senses (seeing, hearing, touching, smelling, tasting) gives us our most reliable form of information is referred to as empiricism.

Empiricism simply means "experience-ism". Modern science is based on the empirical belief that what is true is confirmed or disproved by sense experience. Empiricism has its origins in British and American philosophy. Empiricism is concerned with establishing the truth by means of scientific testing. In other words, empiricism tests, or checks, to see whether what is claimed to be true is confirmed by the way we experience the world through our senses.

One question empiricists ask is "How do I know if something is true?"

Their answer is: "I only know something is true if I have experienced it through my senses."

Their other answer is: "I only know if something is true if I can test it scientifically."

Activity

One of the following statements is not a fact we can check in any way. Which one is it and why?
1. The book I am reading is published in South Africa.
2. Africa is the world's poorest continent.
3. Bertrand Russell was a famous philosopher.
4. Beauty is all around us.
5. It gets dark at about 6 pm in winter in Johannesburg.

Question

1. Doing the shopping one day, you suddenly see a friend on the other side of the shopping mall. You wave and call out. The other person turns towards you and you see, suddenly, that it is someone else.

   What made you think this person was your friend?

   _____

   _____

2. As a child, you put a stick in a pond and the part of the stick in the water "bent". But when you took the stick out of the water, it was still straight.

   What made the stick look bent? Do you know why this happens?

   _____

   _____

3. In the Middle Ages, people thought that the world was flat. When Columbus set sail for America, some of his sailors were frightened that the ship would fall off the edge of the world. Now we all know that the world is round.

   Why do we no longer believe that the world is flat?

   _____

4. Suppose someone tells you that your friend, Lesibe, is a thief. You get angry and tell the person that Lesibe is a decent person you've known for years. You notice, some days after this, that some money is missing from your bag. You remember that the previous day you had lunch with Lesibe and left your bag with him to look after when you went to the bathroom.

   Would this make you believe that Lesibe is, after all, a thief?

   _____

   _____

Thinking clearly and learning from experience

All these scenarios and questions involve finding out, or trying to find out, whether something is true or false.

Just supposing ...

Just suppose you are travelling home alone one night. You've had a hard day at work and you've just had a couple of drinks at the pub. You're feeling absolutely bombed out and a bit drunk. Then, as you pass a piece of empty veld, you notice a saucer-shaped object, brightly lit, stationed on the ground. You stop the car immediately and peer at the object. No doubt about it – it's a flying saucer. You feel terribly frightened and drive off quickly. The next day, you pass the same spot and the veld is empty.

> Did you see a flying saucer the previous night nor not?
>
> **Question**
>
> Suppose, later on the next day, you read in the newspaper that other people had seen flying saucers in the same place recently and that a team of scientists from NASA and Russia are coming to investigate and speak to people about it.
>
> Now do you think you saw a flying saucer that night?

Empiricists claim that experience is the only reality there is. All our knowledge is based on our own experience and other people's experiences. People who promote empiricism tend to be critical of the claims of religion and the claims of ideologies such as Marxism.

Does it work?

What empiricism can help us to do
1. Understand how our physical world operates.
2. Test the truth of certain claims.

3. Refute what is false.
4. Respect the natural laws of the Universe.
5. Learn from experience.

What the failings of empiricism are
1. It places too much emphasis on science.
2. It ignores human values.
3. It views human beings as machines.
4. It tends to ignore anything that cannot be explained scientifically.
5. It confines truth to that which can be experienced through the senses.

Empiricism in a nutshell
Empiricism has its origins in British and American philosophy. Empiricism claims that our most reliable form of knowledge comes from direct experience through the senses.

Empiricism claims that science gives us the most reliable form of truth. If we ignore empiricism, we will fail to learn from our experiences and in the process make ourselves vulnerable to anything that is false. This could have serious consequences. Imagine defying the law of gravity and jumping off a ten-storey building. Experience tells us that if we jump into fresh air we will fall to the ground like a stone. Ignoring this fact would certainly lead to severe injury, if not death itself.

Philosophers at work
Linguistic analysis, logical symbolism and empiricism together formed the school of British philosophy known as logical empiricism (often called logical positivism). Logical positivism thrived during the first half of the 20th century, particularly in Britain and the United States. Today, empiricism is still very much a force in philosophy, but logic less so.

Question

Is logic empirical?

two Asking questions: challenging what the world tells us

Turn on the news and listen for a moment. It can be any news – local South African, CNN, Sky. Or see if you can pick up a phone-in show on the radio and listen to what people say. Listen to what the presenter says. Or look at a newspaper, any newspaper.

Within about five minutes, you will almost certainly hear or read someone else's opinion on some issue, or his or her view of what needs to be done to solve some problem. It may be a problem you've thought about yourself. Maybe you have your own views on the problem.

> **Question**
> Do you think human beings are solving their problems?
> Or is the world getting worse?

> **Question**
> What do you think causes the following?
> - crime
> - violence
> - Aids
> - war
> - poverty

Perhaps you answered "I don't know" to the questions above. If so, you are an unusual person. We say this because most people, certainly most adults, believe they have answers to just about everything. You may well have heard people say things like:
- "If they bring back the death penalty, most crime would stop."
- "Poverty only happens when people don't want to work."
- "Aids is just a scare story."
- "The UN peacekeeping forces can prevent war."
- "Violence is caused by guns. If the government bans guns, violence will stop."

Politicians are always telling us they have solutions. The world over, politicians promise that if they get voted into power, they'll solve just about everybody's problems. Think back to the last election campaign. Who was going to solve what? Did the party who got into power solve any of your problems?

Now read the following, from a book about science:

> In everyday life we want certainty and we invariably view our theories as Absolute Truth. We need solutions right now for the problems of poverty and environmental degradation, or to cure diseases. We cannot afford to wait until the year 2500 for the answer, since failure to act now may find us as extinct as the dinosaur. When a child is sick, we want a cure now, not in half a century's time. But scientists operate on a different time-scale. Their concern is to try and understand how and why the world is as it is; and if this takes 500 years of collective effort by a thousand individuals scattered in laboratories all around the world, so be it ... Success in science comes only from a long slow methodical working through of all ins and outs of a very complex phenomenon, checking and double-checking ... because only by patience and careful testing will we avoid mistakes.   (Robin Dunbar, *The Trouble with Science*)

If human beings have made any progress at all in the last few centuries, it is in scientific discovery. We haven't found a cure for Aids yet, but we know far more about the disease than we did, say, even five years ago.

What is scientific thinking?

Scientific thinking, we believe, is actually an unusual and rare thing. Few of us think scientifically, and this isn't because we aren't scientists, it's because we want to be certain about things. We like to feel we're educated and knowledgeable. We get onto the "information superhighway", the Internet. We read *Time* magazine, books on philosophy and a good newspaper in order to stay informed. We make a point of watching the news on TV.

But are we informed? Do we actually know what's going on in the world around us? In everyday life, we often don't have time to question what we're told. When we were children, we believed what our parents told us, what the pastor told us and what our teachers told us. Now that we're adults, we believe what the media tells us.

Asking questions

Has anyone ever told you a lie? How did you find out?	**Question**

Which political party do you vote for? Do you think this party ever tells lies?	**Question**

Which political party would you never vote for? Why?	**Question**

If you work for an employer, what sort of questions aren't you "allowed" to ask?	**Question**

Developing a questioning attitude is essential in science and is, possibly, one of the main things philosophy teaches us to do.

Activity

We've just asked you to think about which political party you voted for. Now try this exercise: think of the political party you hate the most and ask yourself:

"Why do people vote for this party?"

Ask yourself this question seriously.

Go and read a newspaper that you know supports this party. Read it carefully, especially the editorial. Afterwards, stop and think.

Do you have a better idea now of why people support a viewpoint that is so different from your own? If you like, try religion instead of politics. If you believe in God, try to think why people don't believe in God.

Talk to someone you know who doesn't believe in God or who doesn't go to church. Listen to him or her carefully.

Activity

Next time you're telling someone what you think about something or someone, deliberately stop yourself and say something like: "You know, I could be wrong about this. Forget everything I've just said. I might be talking a load of rubbish. I need to think about this some more."

Try it. See what happens.

Activity

Perhaps you're the sort of person who finds it difficult to talk much, particularly to people who seem very confident or who seem to have all the answers. You may be the sort of person who tends to listen, instead.

Next time, give your opinion and speak your mind. See what happens.

Did anyone try to shut you up? Who?

Asking questions

Just supposing ...

Scenario 1
You're waiting for the taxi that takes you to work every morning. Somebody new is queuing next to you and asks you what time the taxi will arrive. You tell him, "8 o'clock". You all wait and wait and the taxi doesn't come. Finally, a different taxi arrives half an hour later.

> Did you give the new person the wrong information? **Question**

Scenario 2
You see an advert on TV for a cut-price computer. It looks really good and you buy one of these computers the next day. You bring it home and you can't get it to work. You phone the shop and they send their computer expert to help you. He takes one look at your computer and says, "You're going to have problems with this computer. That's why it was cut-price. But I'll do my best." He fixes your computer and it runs perfectly every day from then on.

> Did the computer expert lie to you? **Question**

Scenario 3
Two friends of yours, Steve and Thandi, have been married for over ten years. They have two children they love and everything is fine – they've got a nice house, good jobs. Someone asks you if they are happily married and you say "yes". A week later, Thandi phones you up and says she's getting divorced from Steve.

> Did you tell the truth when you said these people were happily married? **Question**

Activity

Read the above scenarios again carefully. What actually happened in each of them?

Scenarios 1, 2 and 3 are all good examples of people being proved wrong about something. It's not a good feeling to be proved wrong and most of us try to avoid it. As Robin Dunbar says, we all like certainty. But we can never be sure we're right about something. We can only be sure we're wrong about something! Scenario 3 is an example of something that happens a lot. We think we know people and then find out we were wrong about them. We can't even be certain about little things, like the taxi turning up on time.

What's all this got to do with science and philosophy? Well, this is about developing a questioning attitude and admitting that we could be wrong. Both these attitudes are very much the concern of that method of enquiry in philosophy known as critical rationalism.

Philosophers at work

The method of enquiry in philosophy that encourages questioning is called critical rationalism. Another name for it is scientific rationalism. It has a very long history and goes back to Socrates, who lived from 470 to 399 BC. Socrates encouraged us to challenge existing ideas and beliefs by questioning them. The Athenian authorities executed Socrates because he questioned the religious practices of the day (the worship of the gods).

As a method of enquiry in philosophy, critical rationalism encourages open-mindedness. Another way of saying this is that it is anti-dogmatic and anti-authoritarian. Critical rationalism is essential for the future of true democracy.

The whole aim of critical rationalism is to make sure we don't come to believe in an idea that is false: this way, we can find out more about the world we live in and progress in our knowledge.

Critical rationalists emphasise that scientists must be objective. This means that scientists tell other scientists what they think is true and then find out what other scientists say. Maybe the other scientists have done tests that support their discoveries.

Critical rationalism is completely against societies where people can't speak their minds freely and discuss things openly. Only open societies are democratic. Only open societies can solve problems by exchanging ideas and trying out new ones.

Empiricism and critical rationalism are "partners". Both methods of enquiry in philosophy emphasise the need to search out the truth as honestly as possible. Empiricism focuses on searching for objective truth, critical rationalism focuses on avoiding falsity.

People who have promoted critical rationalism:
- Stephen Hawking (British scientist)
- Albert Einstein (German scientist)
- Karl Popper (British philosopher)
- Godwin Sogolo (African philosopher)
- Helen Suzman (South African politician)
- Hannah Arendt (German American philosopher)
- Nelson Mandela (former South African president)

Activity

Read the following statements:

John: "I've never been to the Kruger Park. I wonder what it's really like?"

Shirley: "I used to believe in God, but I'm not so sure now. I've seen too many people suffer."

Thabo: "I vote for the ANC. But I don't agree with all their ideas. I think they need to be more aware of the problems in South Africa today."

Gerrie: "I'm going to the library today to see if I can get a book on gardening. I don't know anything about gardening."

Hester: "I'm an out-and-out Marxist. Marxism has the answers to the world's problems. It's no good listening to capitalists. They don't know what they're talking about."

Question

One of the people above is not a critical rationalist. Which one? Why not?

Our response

It is obvious to us that Hester is the odd person out. She reveals a "know-all" attitude and is convinced of her own rightness to the exclusion of all else. For Hester, there is no question of her being wrong and no hint of questioning her own position.

> I like the idea of a bumper sticker that says, "I may be wrong".
> (Robert Fulghum, in *All I really need to know I learned in kindergarten*)

Question

Have you ever discovered that you were wrong about something? What happened? What did you learn from this experience?

The problem of values in critical rationalism

How do we find out if our values are good or bad? We can ask this question in another way: How do we find out if our morals are right or wrong?

We often hear people say things like:
- "It's wrong to steal, no matter how poor you are. Other people's property should be respected."
- "Criminals are treated too kindly. They should bring back the death penalty."
- "I don't believe in abortion. It's murder."
- "Men and women are equal. I'm glad the new Constitution recognises this."
- But how do we find out whether these ideas are right or wrong?

Morals are not the same as science. Medical researchers are working hard to find out how to cure Aids. They don't have an answer yet, but sooner or later they will – possibly not in our lifetime.

But it makes no sense at all to say something like: "Some people think abortion is wrong. Other people agree with it. We should ask the government to set up a team of scientists to find out who is right here." Or "Some people want the death penalty brought back. We need to get some scientific research going to find out if the death penalty is good or bad."

In other words, morals are not objective. People have different ideas about what is right and wrong.

But the puzzling thing is this: there does seem to be a link between morals and truth.

> **Question**
>
> Supposing you heard someone say the following:
> "What's all the fuss about murder and rape? It's fine to do these things. Too bad if the victims suffer. That's their problem."
> What would your reaction be to this statement?
>
> You would probably think: "This person is sick and needs help."

The truth about what is morally right or wrong is one of the central problems of philosophy.

Critical rationalism says that the best we can do is to be totally democratic and let everyone say what they think about, for example, abortion or the death penalty. During the late 1990s, some people in South Africa believed that a referendum should be held on the death penalty. If more than 50% of the people in South Africa voted for it, then, these people argued, the death penalty should be restored.

Just supposing ...

Suppose you got into politics and got elected as president. One day, a group of people ask to meet you. They call themselves The Critical Rationalist Party. They tell you that they want to see you make more use of referendums for everything, including economic policy. "It's time everyone got a say and not just the politicians", they tell you.

> **Question**
>
> How would you react to this idea of government by referendum?
> Can you think of any problems that might arise?

Thought break

A woman approaches you in the street one day and asks you to sign a petition for free child-care for all working women. You sign the petition, but later on a friend of yours, a man, tells you that free child-care will cost South Africa too much money.

> Would you argue with your friend? Or would you agree with him and wish you hadn't signed the petition?

In August 1999, a BBC news report claimed that Aids figures in America had dropped because of the effectiveness of new drugs and the influence of education.

> Do you think this report applied to the USA only? How would you find out about Aids figures in South Africa?

> What problem in the world upsets you and makes you angry? What do you think should be done to solve this problem?

A friend of yours tells you that her child has incurable cancer. She says the doctor has told her that this type of cancer won't be curable for at least another ten years. She asks you to pray for her child. "Even if science can't help my child, I know God can," she says.

> How would you answer her?

Quick summary

Critical rationalists believe we should question what we're told and that we should carefully examine our own ideas.

Critical rationalists ask one simple question: "Are we sure we're right?" They believe that human beings can solve their problems by thinking clearly and by discussing everything openly.

Critical rationalists focus on one thing: avoiding falsity.

Critical rationalism has much to offer. One of the problems of the modern world is that we tend to simply believe whatever the media tells us. Critical rationalism tells us that we should be far more critical of what the articles in media such as *Time* magazine, *Newsweek*, CNN and Sky News say. The media world is owned by extremely rich, powerful people who may well want us to believe certain things and ignore others. It is probably unwise to rely on just one source for our information.

The same is true of politics. We need to be very careful indeed before trusting what politicians and political parties tell us.

If we believe that the truth is important, critical rationalism will always be part of our lives.

Does it work?

What critical rationalism can help us to do

1. Question what people in authority tell us.
2. Be more open to what other people think.
3. Examine our own opinions more carefully.
4. Be more tolerant and understanding.
5. Solve problems.

What critical rationalism can't help us to do

1. Make quick decisions.
2. Find the meaning of life.
3. Deal with people who are dishonest.
4. It can make us feel insecure.
5. Solve the problem of suffering.

Types of false argument

One of the most useful tools of critical rationalism is its classification of various types of false argument. The most important are name-calling, false cause and effect, falsely representing an opinion, appealing to emotion, and false argument from popularity, described below. Be on the lookout for these arguments next time you hear or read something in the media or if you're in the middle of a discussion.

- **Name-calling.** Attacking the person and not the opinion he or she has. In philosophy, this is called the fallacy of the *ad hominem* argument.

Example: "Sipho says the DA are the best party to vote for, because they have sound economic policies. That's typical of DA supporters: they're all **greedy capitalists**."

Sipho may be a greedy capitalist, and many people who support the DA may be greedy capitalists. But that's got nothing to do with whether or not the DA have sound economic policies.

- **False cause-and-effect.** Falsely claiming that an action has, or will have, a certain effect.

Example 1: "*If* the government bans guns, *then* we'll have a lot less violence in South Africa."

This is a popular, false argument that is particularly favoured by the media. In fact, there is no established link, anywhere in the world, between strict gun control and reduced violence. Nobody knows what causes violent crime in a society.

Example 2: "*If* the government brings back hanging, *then* there will be fewer murders."

Again, this is a popular argument and, again, an argument with no basis. There is no established link between capital punishment and the amount of violent crime in a society. To repeat: nobody knows what causes violent crime.

Example 3: "*If you* join our group, *then you will* become a millionaire within six months. Don't miss this business opportunity!"

This, too, is an argument claiming, falsely, that two things are linked. There are always a number of these "business opportunities" around. There is no established link between joining these schemes and getting rich. In fact, many of these schemes cost money (the joining fee).

- **Falsely representing an opinion in order to discredit it.** In philosophy, this is known as the "straw man argument".

Example 1: "People who say there's no God think it's okay to ignore moral rules."

This is a false argument put forward by some religious groups to discredit non-believers and atheists. First of all, lots of people who believe in God act immorally. Secondly, many atheists place a high value on moral rules.

Example 2: "Christianity claims that God created the world in seven days."

This is a false representation of Christianity put forward by certain secularists and atheists. Christianity, today, covers an extremely wide range of beliefs and opinions and relatively few Christian groups believe this.

Asking questions

▸ *Appeal to emotion (usually, fear).* Appeals to emotion are probably the easiest type of false argument to spot.

Example (political): The people of South Africa have a choice: either vote for our political party or watch the crime rate get worse.

There is no established link between political policies and violent crime anywhere in the world.

▸ *Falsely claiming that, because a point of view is popular, it must be true.*

Example: Our religion is the fastest growing religion in South Africa today: that's because we teach the truth.

The fact that a group of society has lots of members doesn't mean that its teachings are true. Throughout history, many people have believed things that have turned out to be completely false.

Question

What type of false argument is used in the following statements?
1. Thandi says that abortion is always wrong. Who cares what she thinks? Thandi's a religious fanatic. *name-calling*
2. If you put your life savings into a share portfolio, your money will be worth double in a year's time. *False cause-and-effect*
3. Islam teaches that terrorism is morally acceptable. *straw man arguement*
4. Our church is a born-again church. The Bible teaches that if you're not born again, you'll go to hell. God is giving you this opportunity to join us! *appeal to emotion*
5. Most people in South Africa vote for the ANC: that's because the ANC has the best political policies. *argument from popularity*

Our response
1. is an example of name-calling.
2. is an example of false cause-and-effect.
3. is an example of a "straw man argument".
4. is an example of an appeal to emotion (fear of hell).
5. is an example of an argument from popularity.

> **Critical rationalism**
>
> <u>Critical rationalism encourages us to question everything we are told. Critical rationalism constantly asks: "How do we know this is true?"</u>
>
> <u>If we ignore critical rationalism, we will almost certainly become very gullible people who can be manipulated by others. We may even end up being guilty or doing real harm to others and ourselves because we fail to question what people in authority tell us.</u>

Earlier on, we said that critical rationalism and logical empiricism are "partners". Below is an example of how this partnership works in practice.

The following article is taken from the website www.mlmwatch.org:

> Please note: multilevel marketing (MLM) is any form of pyramid selling that involves recruiting other people to sell products. There are a number of multilevel marketing schemes in South Africa today. All of them promise riches to those who join and most of them claim to be based on the teachings of Jesus. However, even a cursory reading of the New Testament makes it clear that Jesus specifically spoke against the pursuit of wealth.
>
> Anybody who invites you to come along to a meeting to hear about "a business opportunity" is probably inviting you to join an MLM scheme. The people running these schemes **want you to believe** that MLM is how all businesses will be run in future. **You will be led to believe** that, if you follow their methods, you will, sooner or later, become a wealthy person. In fact, all MLM schemes are **little more than deceptions that, in the words of the American author Robert Fitzpatrick, "are hidden behind misleading slogans"**. To quote Fitzpatrick again: "Calling it [an MLM scheme – our explanation] a 'great business opportunity' makes no more sense than calling the purchase of a lottery ticket a 'business venture' and winning the lottery a 'viable income opportunity for everyone'."
>
> In **fact**, most people who get sucked into these schemes end up spending far more money on motivation tapes, books, conferences than they ever make out of their increasingly desperate attempts to recruit people. The reason for this is simple: MLMs are based on the **mathematical and logical impossibility of endless growth. No product, not even Coca-Cola, has an endlessly growing market.**
>
> MLMs are attractive to a number of people because they are based on the **comforting, but false, western belief** that if you work hard enough at selling something, you will eventually be rich. One of the **cunning ploys** that the people who run these schemes use is to make sure that newcomers only ever meet the tiny handful of people **(about 1% at most)** who got in early and who did make money.
>
> One of the first things that new and potential recruits are told is that success is easy. Join their scheme and you will end up rich, with lots of friends.
>
> Not only will you not make lots of money, you are likely to lose the friends you do have. Even worse, you may well end up upsetting your closest family. This is because, in

Asking questions

reality, you will find yourself having to put pressure on everybody you know to join, and people resent this sort of thing.

It is also a lie to say that working for an MLM is easy and can be done in your spare time. It is not easy and will probably exhaust you. You will find yourself endlessly trying to recruit (that is, sell) to people. You will also find yourself having to cope with the constant trauma of phoning people you barely know to invite them to join.

This, in turn, will lead to your feeling humiliated. This is the real reason why most people drop out.

To end with another quote from Robert Fitzpatrick:

"In the **logic** of MLM, everyone is a prospect. Every waking moment is a potential time for marketing. There are no off-limit places, people, or times for selling. **Consequently,** there is no free space or free time once a person enrols in the MLM system. While claiming to offer independence, the system comes to dominate people's entire life and **requires rigid conformity** to the program. This is why so many people who become deeply involved **end up needing and relying** upon MLM desperately."

In short, all MLM schemes are destructive cults.

Question

Has anybody ever approached you with an invitation to join one of these schemes? If you're involved with one of these schemes, how much money have you made so far?

three — How in the world can we give our lives meaning?

Some years ago, the following graffiti appeared on a wall in London, England:

WORK EAT SLEEP WORK EAT SLEEP WORK EAT SLEEP. DIE.

On a wall in Sandton, Johannesburg, South Africa, someone asks a question:

WHAT'S IT LIKE TO BE FIFTY, STRESSED AND STILL IN THE RAT RACE?

Question

What do you think these writers are saying? Do you think the writer of the WORK EAT SLEEP DIE graffiti is a happy person, someone who is enjoying life?

What about the second writer? Do you think this writer is part of the rat race?

_____

_____

If someone gave us a wall to write on and a pot of paint, we think our graffiti would say this:

DOES LIFE HAVE ANY MEANING?

CAN WE CREATE MEANING?

CAN WE CREATE OUR OWN LIVES?

Does life have any meaning for you? What do you think life is about? Do you think life is worth living? Do you know anyone who has committed suicide, or tried to commit suicide?

We don't know anyone who has succeeded in committing suicide, but we know a few people who hate life and a few people who have tried to commit suicide. These people are intelligent, educated, "lucky" people, with jobs, cars and houses. But they are not happy people and, despite their education, they don't know why.

One of them attended a funeral recently and said: "I looked at that coffin and thought of the person inside it. I said, 'You're lucky. All your problems are over'."

At the Forum Conference in Prague, in September 1997, the Buddhist leader the Dalai Lama said:

> I believe that the very purpose of life is to be happy. From the very core of our being, we desire contentment. In my own limited experience I have found that the more we care for the happiness of others, the greater is our own sense of well-being. Cultivating a close, warm-hearted feeling for others automatically puts the mind at ease. It helps remove whatever fears or insecurities we may have and gives us the strength to cope with any obstacles we encounter. It is the principal source of success in life. Since we are not solely material creatures, it is a mistake to place all our hopes for happiness on external development alone. The key is to develop inner peace.   (Source: www.tibet.com)

As a young man, the Dalai Lama knew great trouble and difficulty. The communist Chinese invaded his country, Tibet. Tibetan people were killed. He and a few of his followers managed to escape over the border into India. In many of his writings, the Dalai Lama has said that meditation and the interpretation of his dreams enabled him and his few desperate followers to remain calm and evade the Chinese who were after them.

In the West, the American psychologist, James Hillman, said this:

> There is more to human life than theories. Sooner or later something seems to call us onto a particular path. You may remember this "something" as a moment in childhood when an urge out of nowhere, a fascination, said to you, "This is what I must do, this is what I've got to have. This is who I am." The call may not have been this strong, but more like gentle pushings in the stream in which you drifted to a particular spot on the bank. Looking back, you sense that fate had a hand in it.
>
> (from J. Hillman, The Soul's Code)

What do we want to do with our lives? How do we want to live our lives? Many years ago, the philosopher Plato said that the whole of philosophy could be summed up in one question: How should we live?

Another way of saying this is: What is the meaning of life?

You've probably seen bumper stickers on cars and taxis that make statements about the meaning of life or say something about our values. For example: "Life is a bitch and then you die" and "I'm for peace".

Question — Suppose you were asked to design a car bumper sticker. What would your sticker say?

Question — If you own a car, do you have a bumper sticker? What does it say?

If you've got children, or you are in contact with them, for instance as a teacher or kindergarten teacher, you could ask them to come up with some ideas about the meaning of life, even if they can't write yet.

Children often remind adults of the important things in life. In their childlike way they often comment on the meaning of life.

The method of enquiry in philosophy that asks, "What is the meaning of life?" is known as existentialism (existence-ism).

Philosophers at work

Existentialism is found in all cultures. Modern African philosophers tend to be existentialist philosophers. This may be because of the huge problems African countries are facing and because Africa is marginalised as far as the world economy is concerned. This may prove to be Africa's salvation.

In modern times, there have been a number of well-known existentialist philosophers. These include:

- Friedrich Nietzsche
- Jacques Derrida
- Kgalushi Koka
- Jean-Paul Sartre
- Frantz Fanon
- Michel Foucault
- Jean Baudrillard
- Luce Irigaray
- W E B du Bois
- Simone de Beauvoir

How in the world can we give our lives meaning?

Since everybody answers the question "What is the meaning of life?" in his or her own way, all the existentialist philosophers came up with different answers. One of the most interesting of these philosophers was Michel Foucault (pronounced "Foo-coe"). Michel Foucault was a French philosopher who died in 1984. He was extremely concerned about the huge influence modern institutions have on human existence. By "modern institutions" he meant schools, big business, prisons, hospitals (including mental hospitals), the civil service, the police force and, of course, the military and the "big churches" such as the Roman Catholic Church. Foucault said that all these institutions distorted life and destroyed the innocence of the human soul.

How did institutions do this?

Foucault said that human beings are essentially free and unformed. But institutions, even "good" institutions such as schools, force the people in them to conform to sets of rules. In the process, people become uncertain of themselves, afraid and artificial.

And the real problem is that modern life is totally dominated by institutions and by "rules and regulations". We do everything "according to the clock", we feel we have to fit in, be accepted and "be like everyone else".

The question that Foucault poses is: "Are you yourself?"

> How do you feel about your own life? Is there anything in it you would like to change? What?

Question

> Did you have any dreams as a child that you have now given up? Do you still have dreams about what you would like to be and do?

Question

These are some of the things the authors of this book would like to do:
▶ grow exotic roses
▶ fly a kite
▶ own a penthouse flat and a Ferrari sports car
▶ get an outrageous hair cut
▶ tell our enemies exactly what we think of them

35

- shout at the boss
- sulk and stay in bed all day long
- climb Mount Kilimanjaro
- enjoy a meal with good friends
- travel the world
- go on a safari trip through Africa to Kenya
- visit the Great Wall of China
- set up a model train platform.

Activity

What do you think this list says about us?
Draw up your own list and write it in the space below. What does your list say about you, do you think?

_____

_____

_____

The following was taken off the Internet, in 1999. It's an article from the *New York Times* and describes life in any of the world's modern cities.

> We are a culture of racing, panicky white rabbits. Naturally, you've noticed.
>
> You don't just do one thing at a time anymore. You multi-task. In the car you drink coffee, talk on the cellphone and listen to self-improvement tapes. In advanced cases of "hurry sickness", you punch 88 on the microwave instead of 90 because it takes less time to tap the same digit twice. There is a whole function of workers weaned on video games who function at "twitch speed".
>
> Can we go any faster? We're trying …
>
> And what is the price for all this speed? You can't keep up.
>
> "Faster" points to James Burke, a science writer, who predicts, "We will need to reskill ourselves constantly every decade just to keep a job" … There is no time for contemplation. We live life in the fast lane …
>
> A man who is an editor of a magazine is quoted as saying, "I can't stand small talk, waiting in line or slow numbers on the dance floor … It's got to the point where my days, crammed with all sorts of activities, feel like an Olympic endurance event: the everydayathon … I hear an invisible stopwatch ticking even when I'm supposed to be having fun."
>
> Observing us glued to our cellphones or computer and TV screens, a journalist looks for the why, "It is the way of keeping contact with someone, anyone, who will reassure you that you are not alone. You may think you are checking on your portfolio, but deep down you are checking on your existence …'

How in the world can we give our lives meaning?

Question

What's your reaction to this article? Do you "live life in the fast lane"? Do you want to?

Question

What do you think the article means when it says, "… deep down, you are checking on your existence"?

The German philosopher Friedrich Nietzsche said this:

> Behind your thoughts and feelings, my brother, stands a mighty commander, an unknown sage – he is called Self.

Do we want to be "mighty commanders"? In other words, do we want to be in control of our lives, of our own existence?

What do you think is stopping you from being in control of your own life?

The South African performance poet and journalist, Sandile Dikeni, wrote the following poem while contemplating the predicament of his existence. The poem is called *African Worker's Lullaby*.

Look not at me little one
throw those deep sunken eyes
a little far
to the Rolls Royce and limousine
rolling and raving on streets of tar
for my man made ignorance is distant from economics
I have no use for polemics
believe me little one

Cry not at me little one
I am but a poor African
no one listens to me
raise your little finger of anger
to mingle with the wild battling waves

at cool white beaches
where the white masters rave
believe me little one

Beg me not little one
beg me not
I myself have none
a machine battling for survival
since the white man's arrival
with the hunger,
starvation and frustration
apparently
to establish a refreshment station
can you believe this little one?

steal not from me little one
steal not from me
I can direct you to where there is plenty
ask for any bus written city
avoid paying if you can
pay if you possibly can
for your destination, little one
is worth millions of rand
believe me little one

Refuse to die little one
refuse to die
for this gun in my hand
shall bring back the land
I know not much about guns
only that they have done more than nuns
and oh yes they do take away life
only to bring back our lives
'strue little one
believe me little one

A well-known American poet, Raymond Carver, wrote the following poem, during what was a time of distress for him. It is called *Iowa Summer*.

The paperboy shakes me awake, 'I have been dreaming you'd come',
I tell him, rising from the bed. He is accompanied
by a giant Negro from the university who seems
itching to get his hands on me. I stall for time.
Sweat runs off our faces; we stand waiting.
I do not offer them chairs and no one speaks.

How in the world can we give our lives meaning?

It is only later, after they've gone,
I realize they have delivered a letter.
It's a letter from my wife. 'What are you doing there?'
my wife asks, 'Are you drinking?'
I study the postmark for hours. Then it, too, begins to fade.
I hope someday to forget all this.

Question

Which poem do you like most? Why? What do you think this says about you?

Question

Do you think life has meaning? If your answer is yes, what meaning does life have for you?

Some people believe life has no meaning, that it is pointless trying to live a good or worthwhile life. These people are called nihilists.

Philosophers at work

The opposite of existentialism is nihilism. Nihilism means "the philosophy of nothing".

According to nihilists, there is no purpose in life and there is no such thing as the soul. Human beings are tiny bits of nothing in the vastness of the Universe and life is simply a waste of time. We might as well shoot ourselves or jump out of the window. Or get up early every day and go to work if we want to. Who cares? The motto is "So what?". It doesn't matter who we are or what we do.

But nihilism is a strange thing. It can lead to violence and chaos, but it can also free people, particularly people who have grown up in very repressive religious environments.

Also, if Michel Foucault was right, and too many of us are full of rules and regulations, then nihilism can definitely help us change this.

Just supposing ...

A friend of yours has lot of problems, problems she can't seem to solve. Things are going downhill and she seems very depressed all the time. One day, you learn she has tried to kill herself and now she's in hospital, recovering. You visit her in the hospital.

Question: What do you say to her? Should you say anything at all?

Does it work?

What existentialism can help us to do

1. Question other people's ideas and values.
2. Be more open about ourselves.
3. Trust our instincts.
4. Spot fakes.
5. Enjoy life more.

What the failings of existentialism are

1. It may make us too trusting.
2. It can be confusing.
3. It may lead to despair.
4. It may leave us feeling helpless and angry.
5. It may be seriously disruptive.

Quick summary

Existentialists believe that the most important thing we should do is to discover, for ourselves, the meaning of life.

Existentialists do not believe that there is one meaning to life (eg to live for God or the church or some ideology) – far from it. Modern existentialists believe that "our duty" is to decide, for ourselves, what life is about.

Existentialists believe we should repeatedly ask ourselves one question: "Is this how I want to spend my life?"

Thought break

> Ask yourself "Is this the way I want to spend my life?

Another interesting response to the question "What is the meaning of life?" is found in what is known as black existentialism. The scholar Lewis R Gordon, in his collection *Existence in Black: An Anthology of Black Existential Philosophy*, contemplates the situation of black people in the world generally, when he asks the probing question: "What is to be done in a world of nearly a universal sense of superiority to, if not universal hatred of, black folk?" Gordon also makes the claim that the issue of race has emerged, throughout its history, as the question fundamentally of "the blacks" more than for any other group.

Thought break

> How do you respond to Gordon's probing question, "What is to be done in a world of nearly a universal sense of superiority to, if not universal hatred of, black folk?"

> Do you believe Gordon's question is valid, and if so, why?

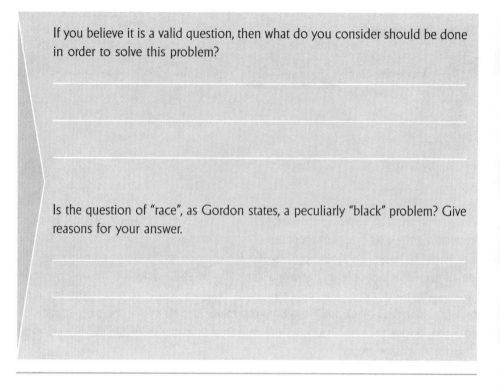

If you believe it is a valid question, then what do you consider should be done in order to solve this problem?

_____

_____

_____

Is the question of "race", as Gordon states, a peculiarly "black" problem? Give reasons for your answer.

_____

_____

_____

Existentialism in a nutshell

Existentialism is that method of enquiry in philosophy that asks: "What is the meaning of life?"

How we approach existentialism depends, to a certain extent, on our culture. People from different cultures will tend to answer the question "What is the meaning of life?" differently.

To some, ignoring existentialism is equal to running the risk of living what the ancient Greek philosopher Socrates called "the unexamined life". The unexamined life, said Socrates, is not worth living. Our lives may be full of activity, but we are likely to experience a certain flatness and staleness. We may find ourselves, when we are older, feeling that life has passed us by.

For the last 200 years, western societies have tended to ignore existentialism in the belief that technological progress could satisfy all human needs. These societies are now paying a heavy price for this delusive love affair with technology: social breakdown, violence, alienation and cynicism are now the hallmarks of the West. Interestingly, a growing number of Hollywood films are now confronting existentialist issues.

four   What of an African world?

What does it mean to say: "I am an African?" What does it mean to live on the continent of Africa, at the beginning of the 21st century? Western economic writers sometimes refer to Africa as "the world's basket case". They point to Africa's wars, starvation, financial collapse and corruption as evidence that Africa seems to suffer from some sort of death wish. In the Western media, the people of Africa are still portrayed as being backwards, as needing the help of the West.

Activity

Wars, starvation and financial collapse. Is Africa the only continent to suffer from these terrible social problems?

Buy a copy of *Time* magazine and read through it. What does it reveal about the social problems Western countries have?

No

Like some great question mark at the centre and crossroads of the world stands Africa. Our best available scientific information tells us that the human race originated there. Probably we humans lingered in Africa for thousands of years before moving off to the ends of the earth, and during that time we developed much that is now common to human thought and life wherever they are found. Africa is then in some sense the mother of us all … indeed, of all civilisation.

(Noel King, in *African Cosmos*)

Rethinking our world

Thought break

When you think of Africa, what thoughts and images come to your mind?
beautiful, hatred, violence, poverty, senselessness, government.

How much do you know about the history of Africa, of South Africa? If the answer is "Not much", where is the best place to find out more?
Does your library stock any books on African history written by black Africans?
What history books did you study at school? Who wrote these books?

Much of the history of Africa has been dominated by colonial occupation. Colonialism in Africa provided the framework for the organised subjugation of the cultural, scientific and economic life of many on the African continent. *[bring under your control, conquer]* This subjugation ignored indigenous knowledge systems and impacted on African people's "way of seeing" and "way of being". In fact, African identity, to all intents and purposes, became an inverted mirror of Western identity. This state of affairs gave birth to numerous attempts to reassert distinctively African ways of thinking and of relating to the world. Such attempts find expression in that spoken tradition and body of literature referred to as African philosophy.

African philosophy

African written philosophy goes back to the time of the pharaohs. Greek and Roman expansion into North Africa produced many African intellectuals, the best known of whom is St Augustine. St Augustine is probably one of the most important people in the Western Christian church. His books *Confessions* and *The City of God* contained some of the key ideas of later Christianity: the belief in original sin, the possibility of salvation through Christ and the Church and the need to work towards establishing

God's kingdom on Earth. In Eastern Christianity, one of the best-known of the desert fathers is the man known as "Moses the Black" who, despite (or perhaps because of) his own violent youth, specifically espoused non-violence, the taming of one's anger (no matter how justified) and harmony.

In the era of post-colonialism (from the mid-20th century onwards) increasing numbers of African scholars felt they had to develop social and economic philosophies that would enable Africa to develop. Given the importance of the community, and the West's destruction of Africa, these scholars rejected capitalism. Instead, they created various forms of socialism which were based on traditional African social and political communalism. Examples are: Julius Nyerere of Tanzania, with his idea of *ujamaa*; Kenneth Kaunda's ideas of Zambian humanism; Kwame Nkrumah of Ghana and Sékou Touré of Guinea, who put forward the idea of scientific socialism; Léopold Senghor of Senegal with his reference to Negritude; and Steve Biko with his reference to Black Consciousness.

The main thing to remember about African philosophy is that it is a response to the problems and troubles of Africa and to the domination of Western thought. African thinkers are keen to disprove the Western belief that Africans are unable to develop a scientific and rational culture. And, at the same time, African thinkers want to confront the question we asked earlier on: what does it mean to say, "I am an African"?

African philosophy consists of the following methods of enquiry:
- ethnic philosophy
- sage (wisdom) philosophy
- political philosophy
- pure philosophy

Ethnic philosophy

Ethnic philosophy can be defined as "the philosophy of Africa. It is distinctive and consists of the religious and moral beliefs of the continent of Africa. Given the vastness of this continent and the diversity of the peoples of Africa, this philosophy should not be simplified. This philosophy contains people's view of life and Africa's ability to criticise its own traditions. Essentially, the philosophy of Africa looks at the "whole" experience of human beings (in other words, the philosophy of Africa is "holistic").

Sage (wisdom) philosophy

Sage or wisdom philosophy focuses on those individuals in society who are known to be wise and far-sighted and who can think critically. These are the people whose views challenge the authority of the community's decision. In the Western version of "wisdom", historically, these people been social critics and innovators.

Political philosophy

Africa's political philosophy is unique. Kwame Nkrumah, Julius Nyerere, Amilcar Cabral, Léopold Senghor and Frantz Fanon are regarded as the main representatives of African political philosophy. The assumption underlying this philosophy is that it must be a peculiarly African political philosophy, different from capitalist, socialist or communist political philosophies.

Pure philosophy

Pure philosophy is philosophy done by African philosophers in the areas we looked at earlier: empiricism, critical rationalism and existentialism. Kwasi Wiredu, Peter Bodunrin, Henry Odera Oruka, Kwame Anthony Appiah and Paulin Hountondji represent this type of philosophy.

Philosophers at work

African philosophy has its roots in a spoken tradition. Written philosophy in Africa south of the Sahara emerged mainly as part of the anti-colonial struggle and the challenges of post-colonial reconstruction. African traditional thought, like classical Western traditional thought, asks the following questions:

- How should we understand the Universe?
- Who and what is God?
- Who is my neighbour?
- What is my duty to my community?
- How should my community be governed and led?

Unlike Western thought, however, which puts the individual at the centre of life, African thought puts the community at the centre of life. This community is not simply the political community – far from it. The African community is much more sophisticated than this: it shares some features with Buddhist ideas of the human community as being a vast, ever-expanding net of spiritual, psychological, biological and emotional relations. The African community, like the Buddhist community, shares the Earth with the unborn, the living spirits of the dead, the Earth, mountains and sky.

African philosophy's impact on Western thought is gaining as Western society becomes more and more troubled, more and more unhappy and more and more fragmented. The New Age movement, despite its name, is an old movement. Its emphasis on our "irrational need" to communicate with the unseen, to learn plant lore (herbalism), to look again at shamanism and to move out into the community of our neighbour owes a great deal to African thought.

People who have promoted African philosophy:
- Kwame Anthony Appiah
- Peter Bodunrin
- Amilcar Cabral
- Frantz Fanon
- Segun Gbadegesin
- Kwame Gyekye
- Paulin Hountondji
- John Mbiti
- Ngugi wa Thiong'o
- Henry Odera Oruka
- Léopold Senghor
- Tsenay Serequeberhan
- Kwasi Wiredu

Ubuntuism

The central ethical idea in traditional African thought is *ubuntu*. The idea of *ubuntu* is related to human happiness and well-being. *Ubuntu* is usually translated into English as "humanity". A fuller meaning of the word *ubuntu* can be found in the Nguni expression *Umuntu ngumuntu ngabantu*. This means: a human being is a human being through other human beings. In other words: "I am because you are." *Ubuntu* avoids the materialism of the Western world. *Ubuntu* recognises that the human self exists and develops only in relationships with other persons.

There are many African examples of *ubuntu*, of caring and sharing, and of forgiveness and reconciliation. The relatively non-violent transition of South Africa from a totalitarian state to a multi-party democracy is based on the values of *ubuntu*. It is a commitment to peaceful co-existence among ordinary South Africans in spite of their differences. *Ubuntu*, argues the South African philosopher Joe Teffo, serves as a cohesive moral value in the face of adversity. Although the policy of apartheid greatly damaged the overwhelming majority of black South Africans, Teffo observes that "… there is no lust for revenge, no apocalyptic retribution. A yearning for justice, yes, and for release from poverty and oppression, but no dream of themselves becoming the persecutors, of turning the tables of apartheid on white South Africans. The ethos of 'ubuntu' is one single gift that African philosophy can be bequeath on other philosophies of the world."

Thought break

> What do you think of the statement: "*Ubuntu* is the one single gift that African philosophy can give to the world"? Do you agree? How has *ubuntu* influenced your life?
>
> _____
>
> _____
>
> _____

Quick summary

African philosophy consists of ethnic, moral, political and wisdom philosophy. It is a response to the problems Africa faces and to the centuries of European domination.

African philosophy is a holistic philosophy which shares certain ideas with Buddhist philosophy: it stresses the importance of the human community and the community's place in the Universe.

African philosophy claims that happiness at least partially consists of living for others, in supporting each other. It is an anti-materialistic philosophy.

Does it work?

What African philosophy can do

1. *Build communities.*
2. *Encourage human beings to be more humble.*
3. *Give us a deeper understanding of ourselves.*
4. *Help us appreciate mystery.*
5. *Re-examine the need for tradition in human life.*

What African philosophy can't help us do

1. It does not challenge power structures.
2. To date, it seems to be unable to accept women as men's equals.
3. It does not encourage critical thinking.
4. It tends to ignore the needs of the individual person.
5. It tolerates cruel superstitious practices (eg burning of witches).

Read the following, which is taken from a speech made by Kenneth Kaunda:

> The Westerner has an aggressive mentality. When he sees a problem, he will not rest until he has formulated some solution to it. He cannot live with contradictory ideas in his mind; he must choose one or the other or evolve a third idea which harmonizes or reconciles the other two. And the Western is vigorously scientific in rejecting solutions for which there is no basis in logic. He draws a sharp line between the natural and the supernatural, the rational and the non-rational, and more often than not, he dismisses the supernatural and the non-rational as superstition ... Africans do not recognise any division between the natural and the supernatural. They experience a situation rather than face a problem. By this I mean they allow both the rational and the non-rational elements to make an impact upon them, and any action they may take could be described more as a response of the total personality to the situation rather than the result of some mental exercise. (Quoted in *Philosophy from Africa*)

Now read this next piece, which was taken from www.kunstler.com. It is an article written by an American writer deeply concerned by the energy crisis and its likely impact on American society. We have shortened and edited this article. We have also highlighted certain words and phrases which we think are highly significant in echoing African philosophy.

PetroCollapse New York Conference
October 5, 2005

Remarks by James Howard Kunstler
Author of *The Long Emergency*, 2005

In the waning months of 2005, our failure to face the problems before us as a society is a wondrous thing to behold. Never before in American history have the public and its leaders shown such a lack of resolve, or even interest, in circumstances that will change forever how we live.
    Even the greatest convulsion in our national experience, the Civil War, was preceded by years of talk, if not action. But in 2005 we barely have enough talk about what is happening to add up to a public conversation. We're too busy following Michael Jackson, or the exploits of Donald Trump. We're immersed in a national personality freak show soap opera, with a "side order" of round-the-clock sports. **Our failure to pay attention to what is important is unprecedented, even supernatural.**

This is true even at the supposedly highest level. The news section of last Sunday's *New York Times* did not contain one story about oil or gas – a week after Hurricane Rita destroyed or damaged hundreds of drilling rigs and production platforms in the Gulf of Mexico – which any thoughtful person can see will lead directly to a winter of hardship for many Americans who can barely afford to heat their homes – and the information about the damage around the Gulf was still just then coming in.

What is important?
We've entered a permanent world-wide energy crisis. The implications are enormous. **It could put us out-of-business as a cohesive society.** We face a crisis in finance, which will be a consequence of the energy predicament as well as a broad and deep lapse in our standards, values, and behavior in financial affairs. We face a crisis in practical living arrangements as the infrastructure of suburbia becomes hopelessly unaffordable to run. How will we fill our gas tanks to make those long commutes? How will we heat the 3500 square foot homes that people are already in? How will we run the yellow school bus fleets? How will we heat the schools?

Some things have already changed as a result of the increase in gasoline prices. American people are increasingly saying: no, we can't afford that new house in Partridge Acres, 34 miles from where we work. And, of course, as the housing bubble deflates, the magical mortgage machinery spinning off a **fabulous stream** of **hallucinated** credit, to be re-packaged as tradable debt, will also stop flowing into the finance sector.

We face a series of ramifying, self-reinforcing, **terrifying** breaks from business-as-usual, and **we are not prepared**.

Mostly **we face a crisis of clear thinking** which will lead to further crises of authority and legitimacy – of who can be trusted to hold this project of civilization together.

Americans have become a nation of **overfed** clowns and crybabies, **afraid of the truth, indifferent to the common good, hardly even a common culture, selfish, belligerent, narcissistic whiners** seeking every means possible to live outside **a reality-based community**.

These are the consequences of a value system that puts comfort, convenience, and leisure above all other considerations. These are not enough to hold a civilization together.

Which is exactly why we have come to refer to ourselves as **consumers**. That's what we call ourselves on TV, in the newspapers, in the legislatures. Consumers. What a degrading label for people who used to be citizens. **Consumers have no duties, obligations, or responsibilities** to anything besides their own desire to eat more Cheez Doodles and drink more beer. Think about yourself that way for twenty or thirty years and it will affect the **collective spirit** very negatively. And our behavior. The biggest losers, of course, end up being the generations of human beings who will follow us, because in the course of mutating into consumers, preoccupied with our Cheez Doodle consumption, **we gave up on the common good, which means that we gave up on the future, and the people who will dwell in it.**

Another obstacle to clear thinking I refer to as the Las Vegas-i-zation of the American mind. The ethos of gambling is based on a particular idea: the belief that it is possible to get something for nothing. The psychology of unearned riches. This idea has now insidiously crept out of the casinos and spread far-and-wide and lodged itself in every corner of our lives.

It's in the rap videos of young men flashing 10,000-dollar watches acquired by making up nursery rhymes about gangster life – and in the **taboos** that prevent us from even talking about that.

People who believe that it is possible to get something for nothing have trouble living in a **reality-based community.**

The Las Vegas-i-zation of the American mind is a pernicious idea in itself, but it is compounded by another mental problem, which I call the Jiminy Cricket syndrome. Jiminy Cricket was Pinocchio's little sidekick in the Walt Disney Cartoon feature. **The idea is that when you wish upon a star, your dreams come true.** It's a nice sentiment for children, perhaps, but **not really suited to adults** who have to live in a reality-based community, especially in difficult times.

The idea – that when you wish upon a star, your dreams come true – obviously comes from the **immersive environment of advertising and the movies**, which is to say, an immersive environment of make-believe, of **pretend**. Trouble is, the **world-wide energy crisis is not make-believe**, and we can't pretend our way through it.

Combine when you wish upon a star, your dreams come true with the belief that it is possible to get something for nothing and you get a powerful recipe for mass delusional thinking.

As **our society** comes under increasing stress, we're liable to **see increased delusional thinking, as worried people retreat further into make-believe and pretend.**

The **desperate** defense of our supposedly non-negotiable way of life may lead to delusional politics that we have never seen before in this land. An **angry and grievance-filled public** may turn to **political maniacs** to preserve their entitlements to the easy motoring utopia – even while reality negotiates things for us.

I maintain that we may see leaders far more dangerous in our future than George W. Bush.

The Long Emergency looming before us is going to produce a lot of **losers**. Economic losers. People who will lose jobs, vocations, incomes, possessions, assets – and never get them back. Social losers. People who will lose position, power, advantage. And just plain losers, **people who will lose their health and their lives.**

There are no magic remedies for what we face, but there are intelligent responses that we can marshal individually and collectively. We will have to do what circumstances require of us.

We are faced with the necessity to downscale, re-scale, right-size, and reorganize all the fundamental activities of daily life: the way we grow food; the way we conduct everyday commerce and the manufacture of things that we need; the way we school our children; the size, shape, and scale of our towns and cities.

These are huge tasks. **How can we bring a reality-based spirit to them?**

I have a suggestion. Let's start with one down-to-earth project that we can take on with confidence, something we have a reasonable shot at accomplishing, and fairly quickly, something that will address our energy problems directly and will make a difference for the better. Let's get started rebuilding the passenger railroad system in our country.

The fact that we are not talking about this shows how deeply unserious we are – especially the Democratic party. I am a registered Democrat. Where is my party on this issue? Where was John Kerry? Where are Senators Hillary Clinton and Charles Schumer? We should demand that they get serious about rebuilding the public transit of America – not next month or next year but tomorrow, starting at the crack of dawn.

Any person or any group who finds themselves in trouble has to begin somewhere. **They have to take a step that will prove to themselves that they are not helpless, that they are capable of accomplishing something, and accomplishing that first thing will build the confidence to move on to the next step.**

That's how people save themselves, how they reconnect with reality-based virtue.

Americans were once **such a people. We** were brave, resourceful, generous and earnest. The last thing **we** believed was the idea that it was possible to get something for nothing. **We** can recover those forsaken elements of our **collective character. We can be guided,** as Abraham Lincoln said, **by the better angels of our nature.**

Question

1. According to the writer, what are the fundamental problems of America?

2. What words and phrases remind you of African philosophy?

3. What words and phrases specifically echo the African concept of ubuntu?

Our response

The writer lists the following as fundamental problems of American society:
1. Superstitious beliefs (eg wish upon a star and your dreams will come true, you can get something for nothing, you can ignore serious problems or treat them as if they don't exist, living in a make-believe world).

2. Greed (eg $10 000 watches)
3. Mass stupidity (*New York Times* talks about Michael Jackson, but doesn't mention the oil crisis once)
4. Mass delusion
5. No sense of collective moral responsibility
6. Growing feelings of fear

The following words and phrases which, as we have said, are the words and phrases of an American writer, remind us very much of African philosophy:
- supernatural (note that this word occurred very early on in the article)
- cohesive society
- common good
- common culture
- the word "we"
- community
- duties, obligations
- collective spirit
- "the people who will dwell in the future"
- taboos
- virtue
- brave, generous
- "We can be guided by the better angels of our nature".

We think the following words and phrases specifically echo the spirit of ubuntu:
- common culture
- common good
- the word "we"
- the entire paragraph about consumerism (which could be paraphrased as "I am a consumer because you are a consumer").

Americans, including the writer of this online article, could reflect on this next piece, written by Kgalushi Koka of the Afrikan Study Programme:

> Why is there a need to find out and know who the Afrikan is? The Afrikan identity is probably wide and varied. Like every living being, the survival instinct of the people of Afrikan descent is emerging quite strongly in an attempt to defeat the onslaught on their personality and the obliteration of the Afrikan's true identity in the circle of the human race.

Thought break

> How do you think African philosophy could help America deal with the problems it is facing?

Read the following two quotes. They both emphasise the importance of community rather than individuality, past and present.

> Our two-million year heritage of hunting-and-gathering life, simple at first but ultimately very complex, left its mark on our minds just as much as it did on our bodies. On top of the technical skills of planning, coordination, and technology, there was, equally important, the social skill of cooperation. A sense of common goals and values, a desire to further the common good, cooperation was more than simply individuals working together. It became a set of rules of conduct, of morals, an understanding of right and wrong in a complex social system. Without cooperation – within bands, among bands, through tribal groups – our technical skills would have been severely blunted. Social rules and standards of behaviour emerged.
> (Richard Leakey, 'The African Anthropologist', in **Origins Reconsidered**)

> Persons are what they are in virtue of what they are destined to be, their character and the communal influence on them ... A person whose existence and personality is dependent on the community is expected in turn to contribute to the continued existence of the community ... The meaning of one's life is therefore measured by one's commitment to social ideals and communal existence.
> (Segun Gbadegesin, in *Philosophy from Africa*)

African philosophy in a nutshell

African philosophy is a complex response to Africa's unique position in the world and human history. It is essentially a form of existentialism.

African philosophy challenges the arrogance of the West and asks the West to rethink its claim of cultural superiority.

If we ignore African philosophy, this means that, in a sense, we are ignoring Africa. We cannot do this without doing some form of inner violence to ourselves, simply because, as far as we can tell, the human race itself became human in

> Africa. There are other reasons why African philosophy cannot be ignored: Africa is a huge continent that contains enormous natural wealth and a growing human population. Africa is part of the world socio-economic order and her philosophy has an impact on that order.

Was colonialism a good thing?

The following is an article written by a rather controversial contemporary writer, Dinesh D'Souza. D'Souza is an Asian American. Again, we have highlighted some words and phrases which we think are significant. Dinesh D'Souza's website is: www.dineshdsouza.com

The Chronicle: 5/10/2002
Two Cheers for Colonialism
By Dinesh D'Souza

Colonialism has gotten a bad name in recent decades. Anticolonialism was one of the dominant political currents of the 20th century, as dozens of European colonies in Asia and Africa became free. Today we are still living with the aftermath of colonialism. Apologists for terrorism, including Osama bin Laden, argue that terrorist acts are an understandable attempt on the part of subjugated non-Western peoples to lash out against their longtime Western oppressors. Activists at last year's World Conference on Racism, including the Rev. Jesse Jackson, have called on the West to pay reparations for slavery and colonialism to minorities and natives of the third world.

These justifications of violence, and calls for monetary compensation, rely on a large body of scholarship that has been produced in the Western academy. That scholarship, which goes by the name of anticolonial studies, postcolonial studies, or subaltern studies, is now an intellectual school in itself, and it exercises a powerful influence on the humanities and social sciences. Its leading Western scholars include Edward Said, Gayatri Spivak, Walter Rodney, and Samir Amin. Their arguments are supported by the ideas of third-world intellectuals like Wole Soyinka, Chinweizu, Ashis Nandy, and, perhaps most influential of all, Frantz Fanon.

The assault against colonialism and its legacy has many dimensions, but at its core it is a theory of oppression that relies on three premises. First, colonialism and imperialism are distinctively Western evils that were inflicted on the non-Western world. Second, as a consequence of colonialism, the West became rich and the colonies became impoverished; in short, the West succeeded at the expense of the colonies. Third, the descendants of colonialism are worse off than they would be had colonialism never occurred.

In a widely used text, *How Europe Underdeveloped Africa*, the Marxist scholar Walter Rodney accuses European colonialism of "draining African wealth and making it impossible to develop more rapidly the resources of the continent." The African writer Chinweizu strikes a similar note in his influential book *The West and the Rest of Us*. He offers the following explanation for African poverty: "White hordes have sallied forth from their Western homelands to assault, loot, occupy, rule, and exploit the world. Even now the fury of their expansionist assault on the rest of us has not abated." In his classic work *The Wretched of the Earth*, Fanon writes, "European opulence has been founded on slavery. The well-being and progress of Europe have been built up with the sweat and the dead bodies of Negroes, Arabs, Indians, and the yellow races."

Those notions are pervasive and emotionally appealing. By suggesting that the West became dominant because it is oppressive, they provide an explanation for Western global dominance without encouraging white racial arrogance. They relieve the third world of blame for its wretchedness. Moreover, they imply politically egalitarian policy solutions: The West is in possession of the "stolen goods" of other cultures, and it has a moral and legal obligation to make some form of repayment. I was raised to believe in such things, and among most third-world intellectuals they are articles of faith. **The only problem is that they are not true.**

There is nothing uniquely Western about colonialism. My native country of India, for example, was ruled by the British for more than two centuries, and many of my fellow Indians are still smarting about that. What they often forget, however, is that before the British came, the Indians had been invaded and conquered by the Persians, the Afghans, Alexander the Great, the Mongols, the Arabs, and the Turks. Depending on how you count, the British were preceded by at least six colonial powers that invaded and occupied India since ancient times. Indeed, ancient India was itself settled by the Aryan people, who came from the north and subjugated the dark-skinned indigenous people.

Those who identify colonialism and empire only with the West either have no sense of history or have forgotten about the Egyptian empire, the Persian empire, the Macedonian empire, the Islamic empire, the Mongol empire, the Chinese empire, and the Aztec and Inca empires in the Americas. Shouldn't the Arabs be paying reparations for their destruction of the Byzantine and Persian empires? Come to think of it, shouldn't the Byzantine and Persian people be paying reparations to the descendants of the people they subjugated? And while we're at it, shouldn't the Muslims reimburse the Spaniards for their 700-year rule?

As the example of Islamic Spain suggests, the people of the West have participated in the game of conquest not only as the perpetrators, but also as the victims. Ancient Greece, for example, was conquered by Rome, and the Roman Empire itself was destroyed by invasions of Huns, Vandals, Lombards, and Visigoths from northern Europe. America, as we all know, was itself a colony of England before its war of independence; England, before that, had been subdued and ruled by Normans from France. Those of us living today are taking on a large project if we are going to settle on a rule of social justice based on figuring out whose ancestors did what to whom.

The West did not become rich and powerful through colonial oppression. It makes no sense to claim that the West grew rich and strong by conquering other countries and taking their stuff. How did the West manage to do that? In the late Middle Ages, say 1500, the West was by no means the world's most affluent or most powerful civilization. Indeed, those of China and of the Arab-Islamic world exceeded the West in wealth, in knowledge, in exploration, in learning, and in military power. So how did the West gain so rapidly in economic, political, and military power that, by the 19th century, it was able to conquer virtually all of the other civilizations? That question demands to be answered, and the oppression theorists have never provided an adequate explanation.

Moreover, the West could not have reached its current stage of wealth and influence by stealing from other cultures, for the simple reason that there wasn't very much to take. "Oh yes there was," the retort often comes. "The Europeans stole the raw material to build their civilization. They took rubber from Malaya, cocoa from West Africa, and tea from India." But as the economic historian P.T. Bauer points out, before British rule, there were no rubber trees in Malaya, no cocoa trees in West Africa, no tea in India. The British brought the rubber tree to Malaya from South America. They brought tea to India from China. And they taught the Africans to grow cocoa, a crop the native people had never heard of. None of this is to deny that when the colonialists could exploit native resources, they did. But that larceny cannot possibly account for the enormous gap in economic, political, and military power that opened up between the West and the rest of the world.

What, then, is the source of that power? The reason the West became so affluent and dominant in the modern era is that it invented three institutions: **science**, democracy, and capitalism. All those institutions are based on universal impulses and aspirations, but those aspirations were given a unique expression in Western civilization.

Consider science. **It is based on a shared human trait: the desire to know. People in every culture have tried to learn about the world.** Thus the Chinese recorded the eclipses, the Mayans developed a calendar, the Hindus discovered the number zero, and so on. But science – which requires experiments, laboratories, induction, verification, and what one scholar has called "the invention of invention," the scientific method – that is a Western institution. Similarly, tribal participation is universal, but democracy – which involves free elections, peaceful transitions of power, and separation of powers – is a Western idea. Finally, the impulse to trade is universal, and there is nothing Western about the use of money, but capitalism – which requires property rights, contracts, courts to enforce them, limited-liability corporations, stock exchanges, patents, insurance, double-entry bookkeeping – this ensemble of practices was developed in the West.

It is the dynamic interaction among these three Western institutions – science, democracy, and capitalism – that has produced the great wealth, strength, and success of Western civilization. An example of this interaction is technology, which arises out of the marriage between science and capitalism. **Science provides the knowledge that leads to invention**, and capitalism supplies the mechanism by which the invention is transmitted to the larger society, as well as the economic incentive for inventors to continue to make new things.

Now we can understand better why the West was able, between the 16th and 19th centuries, to subdue the rest of the world and bend it to its will. Indian elephants and Zulu spears were no match for British rifles and cannonballs. Colonialism and imperialism are not the cause of the West's success; they are the result of that success. The wealth and power of European nations made them arrogant and stimulated their appetite for global conquest. Colonial possessions added to the prestige, and to a much lesser degree the wealth, of Europe. But the primary cause of Western affluence and power is internal – the institutions of science, democracy, and capitalism acting together. Consequently, it is simply wrong to maintain that the rest of the world is poor because the West is rich, or that the West grew rich off stolen goods from Asia, Africa, and Latin America. The West created its own wealth, and still does.

The descendants of colonialism are better off than they would be if colonialism had never happened. I would like to illustrate this point through a personal example. While I was a young boy, growing up in India, I noticed that my grandfather, who had lived under British colonialism, was instinctively and habitually antiwhite. He wasn't just against the English; he was generally against white people. I realized that I did not share his antiwhite animus. That puzzled me: Why did he and I feel so differently?

Only years later, after a great deal of reflection and a fair amount of study, did the answer finally hit me. The reason for our difference of perception was that colonialism had been pretty bad for him, but pretty good for me. Another way to put it was that colonialism had injured those who lived under it, but paradoxically it proved beneficial to their descendants. Much as it chagrins me to admit it – and much as it will outrage many third-world intellectuals for me to say it – my life would have been much worse had the British never ruled India.

How is that possible? Virtually everything that I am, what I do, and my deepest beliefs, all are the product of a worldview that was brought to India by colonialism. I am a writer, and I write in English. My ability to do this, and to reach a broad market, is entirely thanks to the British. My understanding of technology, which allows me, like so many Indians, to function successfully in the modern world, was largely the product of a Western education that came to India as a result of the British. So also my beliefs in freedom of expression, in self-government, in equality of rights under the law, and in the universal principle of human dignity – they are all the products of Western civilization.

I am not suggesting that it was the intention of the colonialists to give all those wonderful gifts to the Indians. Colonialism was not based on philanthropy; it was a form of conquest and rule. The British came to India to govern, and they were not primarily interested in the development of the natives, whom they viewed as picturesque savages. It is impossible to measure, or overlook, the pain and humiliation that the British inflicted during their long period of occupation. Understandably, the Indians chafed under that yoke. Toward the end of the British reign in India, Mahatma Gandhi was asked, "What do you think of Western civilization?" He replied, "I think it would be a good idea."

Despite their suspect motives and bad behavior, however, the British needed a certain amount of infrastructure to effectively govern India. So they built roads, shipping docks, railway tracks, irrigation systems, and government buildings. Then they realized that they needed courts of law to adjudicate disputes that went beyond local systems of dispensing justice. And so the British legal system was introduced, with all its procedural novelties, like "innocent until proven guilty." The British also had to educate the Indians, in order to communicate with them and to train them to be civil servants in the empire. Thus Indian children were exposed to Shakespeare, Dickens, Hobbes, and Locke. In that way the Indians began to encounter words and ideas that were unmentioned in their ancestral culture: "liberty," "sovereignty," "rights," and so on.

That brings me to the greatest benefit that the British provided to the Indians: They taught them the language of freedom. Once again, it was not the objective of the colonial rulers to encourage rebellion. But by exposing Indians to the ideas of the West, they did. The Indian leaders were the product of Western civilization. Gandhi studied in England and South Africa; Nehru was a product of Harrow and Cambridge. That exposure was not entirely to the good; Nehru, for example, who became India's first prime minister after independence, was highly influenced by Fabian socialism through the teachings of Harold Laski. The result was that India had a mismanaged socialist economy for a generation. But my broader point is that the champions of Indian independence acquired the principles, the language, and even the strategies of liberation from the civilization of their oppressors. This was true not just of India but also of other Asian and African countries that broke free of the European yoke.

My conclusion is that against their intentions, the colonialists brought things to India that have immeasurably enriched the lives of the descendants of colonialism. It is doubtful that non-Western countries would have acquired those good things by themselves. It was the British who, applying a universal notion of human rights, in the early 19th century abolished the ancient Indian institution of suttee – the custom of tossing widows on their husbands' funeral pyres. There is no reason to believe that the Indians, who had practiced suttee for centuries, would have reached such a conclusion on their own. Imagine an African or Indian king encountering the works of Locke or Madison and saying, "You know, I think those fellows have a good point. I should relinquish my power and let my people decide whether they want me or someone else to rule." Somehow, I don't see that as likely.

Colonialism was the transmission belt that brought to Asia, Africa, and South America the blessings of Western civilization. Many of those cultures continue to have serious problems of tyranny, tribal and religious conflict, poverty, and underdevelopment, but that is not due to an excess of Western influence; rather, it is due to the fact that those countries are insufficiently Westernized. Sub-Saharan Africa, which is probably in the worst position, has been described by U.N. Secretary General Kofi Annan as "a cocktail of disasters." That is not because colonialism in Africa lasted so long, but because it lasted a mere half-century. It was too short a time to permit Western institutions to take firm root. Consequently, after their independence, most African nations have retreated into a kind of tribal barbarism that can be remedied only with more Western influence, not less. Africa needs more Western capital, more technology, more rule of law, and more individual freedom.

The academy needs to shed its irrational prejudice against colonialism. By providing a more balanced perspective, scholars can help to show the foolishness of policies like reparations as well as justifications of terrorism that are based on anticolonial myths. None of this is to say that colonialism by itself was a good thing, only that bad institutions sometimes produce good results. Colonialism, I freely acknowledge, was a harsh regime for those who lived under it. My grandfather would have a hard time giving even one cheer for colonialism. As for me, I cannot manage three, but I am quite willing to grant two. So here they are: two cheers for colonialism!

Copyright © 2002 by The Chronicle of Higher Education

Thought break

Do you agree or disagree with Dinesh D'Souza? To what extent do you feel that you and the people of your community are influenced by Western science?

five   Can we change our world?

What is "the system"? "The system" is the political, social and economic system we're all caught up in. Why are we all caught up in it? We're not certain. But we need money to buy food, to send our children to school, to get a home loan, to buy clothes, to buy the things we need and the things we want. So we get a job (at least, we hope we do), we put up with it (how many people like the job they do?), and before we know it we're living the message of that graffiti on the London Underground:

WORK EAT SLEEP WORK EAT SLEEP WORK EAT SLEEP. DIE.

Or we're sitting in a car in a traffic jam on a crowded highway with everybody inching forward and a few people weaving in and out trying to get ahead faster. Have you noticed people's expressions in traffic jams?

Or we're sitting in a taxi, in the same traffic jam, wishing that we could afford a car (especially that big, silver BMW in front of us) and then we wouldn't have to sit jammed together will all these other people, especially the woman with the shopping bags and the man who talks all the time.

Or maybe we're the person in that big, silver BMW with leather upholstery, CD/radio player, air-conditioning, automatic windows, looking at that other graffiti:

WHAT'S IT LIKE TO BE FIFTY, STRESSED AND STILL IN THE RAT RACE?

Thought break

Is there a better way to live?

Rethinking our world

> How do you feel about "the system"?
> What do you like about it? What do you hate about it?

This is what we like about "the system". It allows us to:
- choose whatever religion we want (or no religion at all)
- read whatever books we want to
- decide how we spend our leisure time
- buy wool
- indulge in hobbies, such as building model aircraft
- enjoy good wine
- buy African artefacts
- buy Persian carpets.

That is what we hate about "the system":
- going to work every day
- shopping at supermarkets
- traffic jams
- listening to the news on the radio
- being in a rush all the time
- unkind people
- Christmas time
- standing in a queue
- untidiness.

Question

> Where do you think the authors of this book fit into "the system"? Are we at the bottom, the top, or somewhere in the middle?
>
> Where do you think you fit into the system?

Can we change our world?

The capitalist system

The system we have in mind is the capitalist system, also referred to as *capitalism*. But what is capitalism?

Today, the question "What is capitalism?" is, quite simply, impossible to answer. The communist dictator of Cuba, Fidel Castro, has described capitalism as "nothing more than a gambling machine where the poor lose everything". The American writer P J O'Rourke, in his book *Eat the Rich*, tried to find out how the stock market worked and ended up feeling bewildered. The whole network of loans, credits, debts, foreclosures, profits, expected company performance, futures, is huge, baffling and – frightening? exciting? both? neither?

This is O'Rourke's description of a day on the Wall Street Stock Exchange, the centre of it all:

> This is an era of strange fame, but the New York Stock Exchange is an odd star even by current standards. It's just a room, or actually three rooms: the Main Room, the Blue Room and the Garage (it used to be one). These rooms are big, dumpy overlit spaces festooned with coaxial cables and mobbed by gesticulating clerks and hollering middle-aged men all wearing ridiculous jackets and scurrying around with complete absence of dignity. Thousands of telephones ring. The floor is covered with trash. Large boards full of little lightbulbs blink huge strings of numbers. Hundreds of video screens display runic symbols and funny numbers. And above it all, high above the frenzy, is the everchanging stock ticker, a crawling electronic ribbon of gibberish … Behold the hero of the late 1990s …. In the modern-celebrity tradition, money making has re-created itself. It has acquired a new, burnished, lovable image … And nobody knows the stock market. The rise and fall of stock prices prove it … Watching the market all the time doesn't help. When we see the moil and tumult on the exchange floor, we're looking at something we aren't seeing and seeing something that isn't there … In fact, when we own any "financial instrument", what we basically own is an opinion. When the British pound loses its value, the number of pence in a pound doesn't change. We just don't feel the same way about pounds anymore: we're nuts about Euros now … We have an opinion. That opinion is a price. And since prices are constantly changing, our opinion is always about to be wrong … In order to understand the stock market, we have to realise that, like anything else enormous and inert, it's fundamentally stable, and like anything emotion-driven, it's as volatile as hell. Got that? Me neither. Now what about all those people running around on the stock-market floor in a state of utter chaos? There isn't any chaos. The New York Stock Exchange is enmeshed in rules. There are rules about everything … The New York Stock Exchange is one of the most organised places on earth. But the organisation is so complex that I stood, stupid, on the trading floor for two days before I noticed there was any organisation …
>
> The traders are mainly Jewish, Italian and, most of all, Irish … I asked a specialist broker why.
>
> "They were cheap labour," he said.
>
> The Irish were hired as clerks and runners and boys who chalked up prices before video screens were invented. They figured out how the whole thing worked, and they stayed.

Rethinking our world

> "How come there are so few Black and Hispanic traders?" I asked the specialist.
> "They're next," he said.
> And, indeed, many of the nonbroker employees on the floor are black, Puerto Rican, Dominican and so forth. And more than a quarter of them are women …

The New York Stock Exchange is the centre of the world's financial system. What happens on the New York Stock Exchange influences the global economy for better or worse.

But there is something far less controllable that influences the world's financial system – the weather, and the weather is not part of any human system. The weather directly influences global food production. Hurricanes, storms and drought mean crop failure and this, in turn, means that we all pay high prices for our food, no matter where we live in the world. Human beings have no control whatsoever over the climate. South Africa is a particularly good example. If South Africa's main crop, maize, is good, then the country does not have to import food, which means less foreign debt. And maize, in particular, depends on enough rain at the right time. There is nothing any of us can do about this.

We have been talking about systems and their effects. The method of enquiry in philosophy that is concerned with the nature of systems and their effects is referred to as systems theory.

Philosophers at work

Systems theory sees things as a whole rather than splitting things into parts, and also encourages us to keep the objective of a system in mind. In fact, systems theory says that we should approach any problem by asking ourselves the following questions:
- Where does the system fit into the total environment?
- How do the components of the system fit together?
- What helps the system to work and what prevents it from working more efficiently?
- What is the goal of the system?

The most famous systems theorist was Ludwig von Bertalanffy. Bertalanffy was a biologist who came to the conclusion that living organisms had to be studied as a whole and not split up into parts (as is done in Western medicine). Over the years, Bertalanffy developed his theory to the point that he claimed that everything had to be studied as a system in order to gain true understanding. The mistake science had made, he said, was that it had studied parts of systems on their own, and not systems as a whole.

Can we change our world?

Systems theory and ourselves

So far, we've been talking about the economic system. But systems theory is not just about economic and political systems. It can also apply to any system that helps us to understand what makes us human. In the last 35 years, one such system has come to the fore: the enneagram. The origins of the enneagram are not Western science, but various forms of primal and Eastern mysticism. The enneagram is particularly interesting because it is a systematic explanation of what social, economic and cultural systems do to us, as human beings. Also, the enneagram has definite echoes of African philosophy: see, for example, the description of the Type Three personality below and how this echoes the concept of African masks. Also note what we say about ubuntuism in the description of the Type Two personality. Finally, "the system" we are born into necessarily includes our past (our ancestors) and our present family network. In short, our ancestors are part of who we are.

The enneagram and the human personality

The personality system known as the enneagram is the "invention" of a man called Oscar Ichazo. Ichazo was born in Bolivia and moved to Argentina when he was a young man. He spent some time in Asia before establishing a systematic approach to the various ideas and concepts of inner work he had encountered on his travels. His initial system of the enneagram was established some time during the 1960s. The aim of his system is self-realisation and the transformation of human consciousness.

The enneagram can be simplified or made as complex as one wishes. Its roots, as far as researchers can tell, include the mysticism of virtually all the world's major religions, and its numerical component is probably traceable to the work of Pythagoras.

The enneagram system is portrayed as follows:

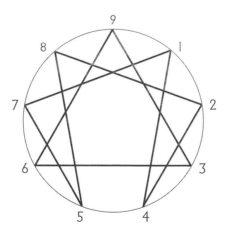

Figure 1: Ichazo's enneagram

The main concept of the enneagram system is that our personalities are distortions of what we really are: these distortions are the result of us having to fit into and survive in, the cultural and social system we were born into. According to some enneagram researchers, sometimes whole societies reflect a specific distortion.

According to the theory behind the enneagram, there are nine main ways in which human beings become alienated from who they really are by the system they were born into. These are:

Type One Personality: the Reformer

The reformer is driven by anger. Type Ones lost their original serenity because the system they were born into violated their integrity.

Their anger causes Ones to feel permanently dissatisfied with themselves and the world around them. Ones work hard to improve themselves as people and to make the world "a better place to live in". Something's gone wrong somewhere, and Ones want to put it right.

Ones remember a time when everything was the way it should be. Their response to life is "Why is there so much wrong in the world? It wasn't always like this! It doesn't have to be this way!"

Ones have a strong sense of injustice and are the people who will "take on" the system. As such, they can be very brave people. In the workplace, for example, if someone is being victimised by the boss, it will be the One who confronts the boss. People like Nelson Mandela tend to be Ones.

Type Two Personality: the Helper

Twos focus on other people. The system made Twos feel they are not essentially lovable people. To get love, Twos believe they have to put others first. They are driven by pride. They are proud of their own "goodness" and willingness to "help out" others. They are often lonely and sad, but too proud to admit this, least of all to themselves. Twos see themselves as loving, kind, well-intentioned people you can always rely on. In a way, the Two appears to exemplify ubuntuism, but the key word is "appears". Unfortunately, in Western societies, Twos often end up as cynical manipulators who put other people in their emotional debt in the vain hope of being loved or simply of getting something out of someone. Twos often immerse themselves in family and social life in an attempt to cover up their loveless state. At their best, Twos genuninely do love others and give selflessly: an example is the late Mother Theresa.

Type Three: the Movie Star

Type Three is particularly important because in Western, image-dominated societies, it is the personality type that is most rewarded and encouraged. Threes learned that in order to survive they had to impress the people around them. Of all the types, these people are the least "real" and most aggressive. Fashion models and film stars exemplify Type Threes. These are the "mask-wearers" whose masks, tragically, have become their faces. Threes are driven by vanity. Threes know that the world they were born into is a world of lies. The authenticity of the Three was threatened and he or she no longer knows who he or she is.

Threes are not necessarily physically beautiful people – they are "show people". They have charisma and they will use whatever gifts they have as a means of putting on a performance. In a way, outcomes-based education is a form of performance ("Show me how clever you are and then I will reward you").

At their best, Threes make the people around them feel good about themselves and they often communicate a therapeutic form of energy, making others want to be like them or even touch them. Jesus of Nazareth may have been a Three. The late Pope John Paul II was probably a Three.

Type Four: the Individualist

Fours know that the system has robbed them of their authenticity. They feel this loss keenly, a feeling which manifests itself as envy of others and, indeed, Fours are driven by envy. Fours are essentially sad people. Why is it that everybody's having a good time except them? Why does everybody else have a wide circle of friends and lots of invitations to parties? They don't know, and they've given up trying to find out. So, to compensate, they glory in their own uniqueness and pain. Fours suffer from a terrible sense of inner lack and may be rather cruel people to deal with. Fours are the depressives that medical science cannot help. Artistic people are often Fours. Picasso was probably a Four. Fours do, in fact, have much to offer because they are so very different: a good example is the philosopher Nietzsche.

Again, the Four is a significant personality type because the Western world claims to be individualistic. In fact, though, Western society is highly conformist and what is regarded as "individualism" is usually little more than sheer ruthlessness.

Type Five: the Scientist

Fives find the system they were born into extremely frightening. Fives feel helpless and are afraid they "won't make it". Fives are trying to recover an original, contemplative, calm, Buddhist-like non-attachment. This manifests itself, ironically, as a craving for more and more knowledge. Fives are driven by greed, by a clutching, mean approach to life and other people. What knowledge they do have they intend to keep to themselves.

Fives are convinced that they must grab what knowledge they can and then rush down into a hole to escape from the reality of the system, a reality which, to them, feels like a freezing winter with no hope of spring. Once they know enough, they think, they will have the courage to "come out of their holes" and confront the system and the people in that system. They can become weird and secretive. Sensible, balanced Fives, however, are invaluable people to know. For example, they often notice things that the rest of us don't and they can be very astute about themselves and others. In a way, the whole thrust of information technology is based on a Type Five approach to life.

Type Six: the Loyal Supporter

Sixes are particularly relevant to any discussion of systems theory because it is the Six who, early on in life, lost his or her faith in "the system" (the system here being the network of adults responsible for looking after the young Six). Somebody has let Sixes down and the Sixes are trying to find something else to replace that "somebody". As a result of their early loss of faith, Sixes are driven by fear. Sixes need some form of inner guidance that will enable them to stop feeling so fearful of the future. That's why many Sixes end up as loyal supporters of systems, be these systems a religion, a political party or a big employer. Such places give them support and provide them with moral and, often, practical guidance. The problem that Sixes have, though, is that they tend to end up terribly dependent on such organisations, which, ironically, makes them even more emotionally vulnerable.

This constant background of anxiety drives Sixes to organise and systematise their environment as much as possible so that it will be predictable and thus less threatening, but this activity does not ultimately reduce their fear.

Type Seven: the Pleasure-seeker

Sevens have had to cope with extremely painful experiences inflicted on them by the system. Such experiences might have included the loss of one or both parents, possibly physical pain, or any form of more or less serious trauma, including hunger and/or extreme poverty.

Sevens believe that the world is full of wonderful things and their task is to grab as many of those wonderful things as possible. In their avoidance of any form of pain, Sevens are, in a sense, "on the run". They are empty people who seek externals to fill them. They can be immoral. Sevens love excitement and will happily take risks. If Sevens ruled the world, none of us would have to work for our living or go to boring school and university. We certainly wouldn't read books like *Rethinking our World*. The capitalist system we referred to earlier on is a perfect reflection of what Sevens believe in: shopping, movies, casinos and ice-cream sundaes. A Seven can be a wonderful person to have around: at their best, they enjoy life and they will go out of their way to give others a good time, too.

Type Eight: the Achiever

Eights are the people who lost their innocence. The world, the system they were born into, revealed itself as ruthless and uncaring and this is a lesson they have remembered in earnest. In a sense, Eights are out to get back at the system and, by implication, at other people generally. Eights are driven by an addiction to power. As a result, they are intense, energetic and domineering. These are the people who simply don't believe in slowing down and letting things be. Historically, in South Africa, it was the Eights who, within the space of little more than 50 years, gained control of the mines in the last part of the 19th century. Any serious power struggle, including a war, usually involves a fight between people who are Eights and who are prepared to sacrifice others to get their way. But it would be incorrect to think that all Eights are bad people. Far from it. Eights can be people with vision. Eights are the people who get things done, who achieve things, who won't give up. Indeed, a healthy Eight will fight tirelessly for, say, democracy and human rights and will use his or her power to protect the weak and the vulnerable.

Type Nine: the Peacemaker

Nines are the people who learned that, in order to survive in the system, they had to be invisible. Paradoxically, Nines are driven by laziness. Nines are the "peace at any price" people, the people who "swing along" with others, who blend in with the crowd. Harmony is important to them because, in a way, harmony is a form of invisibility and it's so much easier not to put up a fight. Nines often give one the impression that they aren't "all there". The sadness of the Nine is that the system made them feel they weren't at all important and that their needs didn't matter. Nines have reacted to this message by feeling that most things are too much trouble. Nines will put off doing things for as long as possible. Nines are asleep to their own lives and themselves as individuals. So long as they can either be invisible or fit in somehow, Nines are happy. Nines are problem-avoiders who hope that things will somehow sort themselves out.

Nines want to remain in some sort of inner world where they feel secure and comfortable.

Nines, in fact, seek union and are often attracted to aesthetic pursuits such as philosophy, poetry and various forms of spirituality.

Nines are definitely needed in our busy, noisy, bustling world of activity and achievement. For a start, Nines are gifted peacemakers – they hate any form of violence and, interestingly, will work hard to restore or create equilibrium and harmony where neither existed. The achievements of the Truth and Reconciliation Commission are a good example of a Nine person, in this case Bishop Tutu, at their best.

Question

1. What personality type do you think you are?

2. In your opinion, what is the personality type of Western societies?

3. How would you describe the personality of Africa?

4. What do you think is the personality type of South Africa today?

Our response
1. Only you can decide this.
2. We think that Western societies are basically Eights, but some enneagram scholars believe that America is a Type Three society because of its obsession with image and performance.
3. We're inclined to view Africa as a Nine society – see, for example, Kenneth Kaunda's remarks about problems in the previous chapter. Of course, you may disagree. If you do, try to say why.
4. South Africa is, we think, also a Nine society but is being forced by the global system to change. This may be the reason for its violence. We don't know.

Just supposing ...

Just supposing you ruled the world ...

Question

What, if anything, would you do about the global capitalist system? Would you try to change the system in any way? How?

Philosophers at work

The concern with changing a system or beating the system, be it economic, social or political, is reflected in the method of enquiry in philosophy referred to as critical theory.

Critical theory is a method of enquiry which has its origins in German philosophy, in the 1930s. The people who first got involved in critical theory were mainly concerned with the problems of Nazism – many early critical theorists were Jewish people. But from the beginning, critical theory was not just about trying to resist the Nazis. Critical theory believes that any form of power structure is dangerous and destructive. Critical theory claims that power structures do not just drive our economic and social life, they actually influence the way we think.

The most famous version of critical theory is Marxism. This is because Marxism, true Marxism, wants to abolish all inequalities of wealth and all social inequalities. Marxists, and all critical theorists, believe that we shall never experience happiness while we continue to be dominated by powerful people and powerful economic systems that trap us.

In short, critical theory can be said to be a form of social criticism.

Critical theory influences a number of philosophies and ideologies. These are:

- Marxism
- Feminism (women's rights)
- Black rights movements
- Some postmodernist thinking
- Socialism.

People who have promoted critical theory:
- Jesus of Nazareth
- Karl Marx (social theorist)
- Gautama Buddha
- Moses
- Mohammed
- Michel Foucault (philosopher)
- Paul Freire (president of Cuba)
- Leon Trotsky (Russian revolutionist)
- Jürgen Habermas (social theorist)
- Most feminists
- Frantz Fanon (African social theorist)
- Amilcar Cabral (African philosopher).

Religious leaders and social criticism

Buddha – Gautama Buddha was the founder of a way of life known as Buddhism. Buddha himself was born into a wealthy family, but he rejected the social caste system of India at the time and left behind his own life of ease and comfort to confront two questions: "Who am I?" and "What is the world?" Strictly speaking, Buddhism is not a religion, but a fairly sophisticated and complex search for reality using, primarily, the powers of the mind. Buddhism rejects any form of violence, including the violent overthrow of unjust social orders. Nevertheless, Buddhism's eightfold path gently and persistently insists that all human beings should work towards creating a new world. This path consists of:

- Right thinking
- Right attitude
- Right means of earning a living
- Right conduct
- Right views
- Right speaking
- Right effort
- Right concentration.

Above left: Jesus of Nazareth; above right: The grave of Karl Marx; below left: An atist's impression of Moses; below right: Buddha.

Today, Buddhism is strongly critical of militarism, Western consumption patterns, economic greed and the sheer frenetic activity of Western life that is being imposed on peoples throughout the world.

Moses – One of the people who can be said to have contributed to the formation of the Jewish religion was Moses. As far as social criticism is concerned, Moses and the liberation of the Hebrew slaves were the focus of liberation/Marxist theology during the 1970s and 1980s. The story of the Hebrew slaves' liberation from social oppression under Pharaoh, and the flight into the Promised Land is, in effect, a community's search for a "better tomorrow". The religion that Moses founded is based, like Islam, on a call for social justice under the One God.

Mohammed – Mohammed's call to be the Prophet of Allah had, as its basis, his radical criticism of the social and economic inequalities of Meccan society at the time. Mohammed passionately believed that all human beings – men and women – were created by Allah and that all are equal before Allah and that He is lord over creation and human life. Mohammed threatened the wealthy Meccan elite by denouncing any form of monetary trickery (eg unjust interest rates), the hoarding of capital and the exploitation of the poor (he showed particular concern for the plight of impoverished women). His vision of society was of all humankind united under Allah. His early converts were poor middle-class artisans and ex-prostitutes.

Jesus of Nazareth – One of the most famous of all religious leaders was Jesus of Nazareth. What do we know about him? He was born about 2000 years ago and died in about the year 30. He is mentioned twice in Roman literature and once by the Jewish historian, Josephus. Josephus's account of Jesus reads as follows:

> At this time there appeared Jesus, a wise man. For he was someone who did startling deeds, a teacher of people who receive the truth with pleasure. And he gained a following among many Jews and also among many Greeks. And when Pilate condemned him to the cross because of the accusations the leaders brought against him, those who had previously loved him did not cease to do so.

Apart from this brief account, there are the first three gospels of the Christian Bible and the Gospel of Thomas. The Gospel of John is a theological reflection on Jesus's ministry.

Jesus's main contribution to religion was his radical criticism of oppressive social and economic structures and his single-minded focus on what he called "the kingdom of God". He insisted that we should forgive and love those who seek to destroy us and he insisted that wealthy people should give away their wealth to the poor. If he hated anybody, it was the smugly self-righteous religious men who dominated Jewish religion at the time and who often personally benefited from existing social arrangements. His followers consisted of people who had been excluded from society: labourers, prostitutes, tax-gatherers. He condemned violence and was eventually put to death by the Roman authorities for encouraging social unrest.

Karl Marx – Another famous critical theorist, though not a religious leader, was Karl Marx. What do we know about him?

Karl Marx was born in Prussia in 1818. His father was a successful Jewish lawyer who became a Christian in 1824, probably because of the anti-Jewish feelings that had always characterised central Europe. Karl Marx studied law at university and became a follower of the philosopher Hegel. Unfortunately, Hegel lost all influence when Friedrich Wilhelm IV came to the Prussian throne in 1840 and this, in turn, destroyed Marx's academic career. Two things resulted from this: Marx became hopelessly poor, and he tried to recuperate his losses by gambling, but failed and fell into the hands of loan sharks. The persecution of his father and the oppression of the Prussian monarchy undoubtedly had a long-lasting effect on his view of society and on the evils of power.

In fact, evil power structures were responsible for the persecution of Marx and his wife, Jenny, throughout their lives. Europe, during Marx's lifetime, was still in the hands of corrupt monarchies. The Industrial Revolution led to unemployment for many and made a few wealthy. After being forced to leave Prussia for his radical views, Marx went to Germany, France and, finally, England. England tolerated him, but no more. He and Jenny lived in dreadful poverty in London and were only saved from starvation by the kindness of his wealthy friend, Friedrich Engels. During his time in England, Marx and Engels visited the cotton mills and both were horrified by what they saw. Wealthy men who employed working-class people (men, women and children) ran the cotton industry paying pitiful salaries. There were no labour laws to protect workers. People were forced to work as much as fourteen hours with no proper toilet or eating facilities. Children working in these places were often permanently crippled from stooping over the weaving machines and it was by no means rare to lose fingers and hands when working the steam-driven machinery. For many people, Marx and Engels were the two men who, in the 1800s, stood for hope and a "better tomorrow".

Karl Marx's most influential work is *Das Kapital*. His most famous and popular is *The Communist Party Manifesto*. The Manifesto is simple in its aims:

QUESTION: What is the aim of the Community Party?
ANSWER: To organise society so that every member of it can develop and use all his abilities and powers in complete freedom and without hurting society.
QUESTION: How do you wish to achieve this aim?

Can we change our world?

ANSWER: By the elimination of private property and its replacement by community of property.

Karl Marx died in London in 1883.

Question

We've just discussed two men: Jesus of Nazareth and Karl Marx. Do you think churches support Jesus's idea about society? If you go to church yourself, does your church reflect Jesus's view of society?

Do you agree with what we've said here about Jesus? If not, refer to the gospels of the Christian Bible and see if you can find support for your idea of Jesus. What is your view of Jesus?

Do you admire Karl Marx? Do you personally want to see private property abolished, and if so, why?

Who do you think has power in South Africa today?

The shape of power

The question of power and who is exercising power is one of the central concerns of critical theory.

One of the characters in Stephen King's novel *It* is an eleven-year-old boy, Ben, who is bullied at school. In this next paragraph, Ben is lying awake one night, thinking.

Rethinking our world

But there would be odd moments of time when he pulled the questions out again and examined them: The power of the silver, the power of the bullets – where does power like that come from? Where does any power come from? How do you get it? How do you use it?

It seemed to him that the lives of him and his friends might depend on those questions. One night as he was falling asleep, it occurred to him that there was another question, perhaps the only question. It had some real shape; he had nearly seen it. To see the shape was to see the secret. Was that also true of power? Perhaps it was. For wasn't it true that power, like *It*, was a shape-changer?

What, exactly what, was power, anyway?

Question   Can we answer Ben?

The French philosopher, Michel Foucault, saw how the shape of power changes. We have already pointed out that Foucault was extremely concerned by the power of institutions such as schools, churches and big business.

If "to see the shape was to see the secret" of power, then we need to follow Foucault's ideas about power and how power is formed in more detail. Foucault claimed that by insisting that people follow rules and regulations, institutions force people into being artificial. But that is only the beginning of it, according to Foucault, because all organisations and institutions do not stop at this. They invade our very selves. How? By forcing us to see life, and to live life, in a certain way.

By "forcing", this does not mean that institutions use some form of physical force, such as caning disobedient children or assaulting adults (although physical force is, of course, very much part of all prisons).

What institutions do all the time, said Foucault, is set up a complex and highly effective spy network. All institutions spy on, and write reports about, the people who are in them. This starts at school. In Western-style countries, parents are legally obliged to send their children to school from the age of about six onwards. In fact, many children now start school even earlier – at kindergarten. Teachers and professional child-minders endlessly monitor the child – and not just in terms of the child's academic achievements. Comments on the child such as the following are regarded as perfectly acceptable and, in fact, desirable:

> ▸ "Ntandi is a quiet, hard-working child who achieves good grades. She is becoming better at certain sports, but she still needs to participate more in group activities. She is still too withdrawn."

- "Karl needs to calm down and work more consistently. He is a bright boy, but apt to jump from one thing to another. He does well in Art, but his Maths is poor. He needs to work on this."
- "Janet is a popular, clever student who seems to get on well with everyone. She is likely to be voted head student next year. She seems to have overcome her problem with exam nerves – the school therapist's intervention probably helped but Janet must also take credit too."

What's actually going on here? What is happening is that the school is monitoring and commenting on three students. In doing so, it's asking Ntandi, Karl and Janet to "do something" about certain aspects of their personalities which the school feels are not quite right. Ntandi is a quiet girl who needs to be more outgoing. Karl is too noisy and needs to be more like Ntandi. And Janet has overcome a previous personality problem. It seems as though the school has an ideal "model" child in mind.

> **Question**
> What does this "model" child look like?

In the West, which is in the process of imposing this ideal on countries such as South Africa, the ideal child has the following attributes:
- is clever
- helps other people
- comes to school clean and neat
- has personal goals.
- makes friends easily
- co-operates in class
- does his/her homework

In other words, the ideal child/student is the one who fits in nicely with the school's system. The opposite of this is the "weirdo/misfit". These are the children who are constantly told that they need to change their attitudes. Very often, these children come from "problem homes" (where they are exposed to alcoholism, divorce, drugs, etc.).

Although this image of the ideal child seems reasonable enough, the worrying thing is that this constant message of "we are watching you and we think you need to do something about yourself" never really stops. You get it while you're at school, while you're at college and if or when you go to work for a large employer. The significant thing, though, said Foucault, is this: eventually, we constantly monitor and evaluate ourselves. "How am I doing?" is the anxious question Westerners are obsessed with. "Am I doing okay with my kids/marriage/job/sex life/finances?" This becomes "Am I doing okay with me?" The answer is nearly always: "No."

And the reason the answer is nearly always "no" is that it is usually not clear to us exactly what we are supposed to be and it is not clear to us who is making these demands. As Stephen King says, the shape of power changes. It changes subtly, gradually or sometimes suddenly. What seems to work for us one day doesn't seem to work the next. We often feel helpless.

How can we "see the shape" of power?

> The new methods of power are not ensured by right but by technique, not by law but by normalisation, not by punishment, but by control, methods that are employed on all levels and in forms that go beyond the state and its apparatus.
> (Michel Foucault, quoted in *Foucault for Beginners*)

What is "normalisation"? Let's ask a simpler question: What is normal? The dictionary helps here, we think:

> Something that is normal is something that is usual and ordinary, in accordance with what people expect.

So is it other people's expectations that form the shape of power?

Thought break

Who and what has power over you right now?

What frightens you? Who frightens you?

Quick summary

Critical theory is the method of enquiry in philosophy that radically questions existing social, political and economic systems. Marxism is a form of critical theory.

Critical theorists tend to be philosophers who have been "hurt" by the system, or who have seen other people hurt by the system.

Critical theorists believe that all forms of power are oppressive.

Some modern critical theorists believe that it is the way we see things that is the cause of our power or powerlessness.

Just supposing ...

Just suppose you had total power over your enemies ...

Question

What would you do to them? You don't have to be nice about it – no one is going to see your answer.

Who do you think might be watching you now?

Do you ever dream of running away? In this dream, where do you run to? What are you running from?

Does it work?

What critical theory helps us to do

1. Realistically assess power.
2. Identify those who have power and those who don't.
3. Identify weaknesses in existing power relations.
4. Define our own, personal power and weaknesses.
5. Re-examine our priorities.
6. Re-assess our lives.

Where critical theory fails
1. It can become fanatical.
2. It is sometimes too simplistic in its analysis of power.
3. It can be too idealistic.
4. It may lead to despair and violence.
5. It tends to ignore human emotions and desires.
6. It can be a very grim philosophy.

Creating power

Milan Kundera, a writer and thinker, was born in Czechoslovakia but had to leave his country because of the oppressive power of communism. In his book *The Unbearable Lightness of Being*, he asks us a fundamentally simple question: how much "weight" do we give things? In other words, how much do we care?

If we care a lot, he says, we will experience two things: life will be difficult, heavy, intense – but it will be real and truthful, to us at least.

Or we can take the other way – the way of "lightness". In this way, we simply choose not to care. Or to care as little as possible.

If we become light, we will also have experiences: life will be easy, and we will be childlike, laughing – but nothing will be real or true.

Thought break

> Can we possibly create power by becoming light and yet be true and real?

Now read the following:

> Anyone who thinks the Communist regimes of Central Europe are exclusively the work of criminals is overlooking a basic truth: the criminal regimes were made not by criminals but by enthusiasts convinced they had discovered the only road to paradise. They defended that road so valiantly that they were forced to execute many people. Later it became clear that there was no paradise, that the enthusiasts were therefore murderers.
>
> Then everyone took to shouting at the Communists: You're the ones responsible for our country's misfortunes (Czechoslovakia had grown poor and desolate), for its

loss of independence (it had fallen into the hands of the Russians), for its judicial murders!

And the accused responded: We didn't know! We were deceived! We were true believers! Deep in our hearts we are innocent!

(Milan Kundera, in *The Unbearable Lightness of Being*)

Thought break

What is oppression?

Jacques Derrida and the power of Western democracy

The well-known French philosopher, Jacques Derrida, died in October 2004. During his lifetime, Derrida expressed a great deal of concern at the smug arrogance of the West. Although he recognised the failure of Eastern communism, he became convinced that the West was far too confident in its power to shape and change the world "for the better".

First of all, democracy had turned out to be very undemocratic. About the only people who have any influence on what happens at government level are politicians and, as we all know, politicians are corrupt liars whose aim is to stay in power and achieve their own ends. Politicians betray the people who vote them into power, but nobody knows what to do about it. Voter turnout in First World countries, particularly Britain and America, is low.

So why are Western democracies failing? Jacques Derrida claimed that Western democracy is failing because it is based on certain assumptions that may be false. These assumptions are that the notions of freedom, justice and equality are simple ideas that can be defined in words – for example, in documents such as the American Declaration of Independence and South Africa's Constitution of 1996.

Derrida said that the problem with such documents was that words and ideas can never be fixed in this simple way. This is why democratic countries have so many social problems (eg crime, greedy and unjust legal systems, broken homes, an increasing wealth gap, etc). Derrida said that people in the West had relied too long on words in documents to work some sort of social magic. The simple fact of the matter is that there's a big gap between words on a piece of paper and what really happens.

Since 1996, South Africa has, in many ways, adopted a Western political ideology and has uncritically accepted many Western ideas. If the West is stuck, and it does seem to be, then we need to listen carefully to what the late Jacques Derrida said.

Derrida believed that words, especially words in political and legal contracts, are somehow dishonest because they replace our human need for trust and openness towards each other. They also replace our moral duty to open our hearts and souls to what he calls "the other", that is, the other person.

This may seem rather vague, so consider a concrete example of what Derrida meant. Take the example of affirmative action in a big South African institution.

All South African employers have a written affirmative action policy that gives priority to black candidates applying for jobs. This is based on justice: black people had no chances in the past, so now South African employers must give black people "more chances" to succeed economically. But you cannot just write out a legal document such as an affirmative action policy, tell management what percentage of black employees it must have by a particular year and then dust your hands, saying, "well, good, now we've got that one right". This approach takes justice and turns it into a legalistic number game, as if black people and white people were just numbers. It's dehumanising.

You need an affirmative action policy but, while making sure that black people get their due, you also need to make sure that white minority groups are not embittered. This depends on people trusting each other. It means going beyond the letter of the law and working out, fairly, what happens in the real-life world of employment and economics.

So, for Jacques Derrida, beating the system and recreating our world depends on trust, openness, faith in each other and admitting that we don't have all the answers neatly calculated in words and numbers.

Derrida was at the forefront of the philosophical movement known as deconstruction. If you are interested in knowing more about it, you can read the following book: Caputo, J D. 1997. *Deconstruction in a Nutshell*. New York: Fordham University Press.

Another book on Derrida, which you might like to buy, is: Collin, J & Mayblin, B. 2005. *Introducing Derrida*. Trumpington: Icon. There are also various Internet sites devoted to the work of Derrida.

Ken Wilber and systems theory

In the last 10 years, a new thinker and philosopher has brought his own ideas to systems theory: Ken Wilber.

Ken Wilber started writing and publishing in the 1970s, but his ideas were regarded as so odd that traditional academia rejected him. Wilber is a Westerner, an American. Originally, he studied microbiology, but he quickly became disillusioned with the scientific/medical establishment which, he claims, tends to treat suffering human beings as objects in a laboratory. Wilber realised that this view of human beings is inevitable because Western thought remains dominated by empiricist concerns that minimise humankind's search for meaning. Given this, when he first started his own research, Wilber's most pressing concern was to see whether empirical science could be harmonised with religion. This, in turn, led to him making a prolonged and in-depth study of Buddhism and eventually led Wilber to formulate a "theory of everything".

The key to Wilber's thought is his rejection of all forms of fragmentation and his conviction that we need a "pattern that connects". The problem with all the forms of philosophy discussed so far in this book is that **they are all only partial truths, but they all claim to be the whole truth.**

Wilber brings all philosophies, all religions, into one. This one he calls "the holon".

Wilber's holon is unique in human thought because it claims that all forms of reality have an "inner" and an "outer", an individual aspect and a social aspect. This is what Wilber's basic holon looks like:

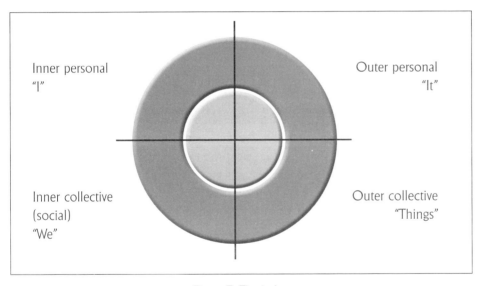

Figure 3: The holon

In other words, we are looking at four quadrants.

According to Wilber, anything and everything can be seen as a holon. You are a good example of a holon.

Left-hand upper quadrant: you have your inner personal world of your thoughts, feelings and dreams (Wilber calls this the "I" quadrant).

Left-hand lower quadrant: your culture, your mutual understanding with the people around you (Wilber calls this the "we" quadrant).

Right-hand upper quadrant: your personal outward appearance, what you do, the answers you give on, say, a job application form (Wilber calls this the "it" quadrant).

Right-hand lower quadrant: the socio-economic system which impacts on you and all of us the whole time. This is the least personal of all quadrants. (Wilber calls this the "its" quadrant. He has also called it the "things" quadrant.)

Holon of philosophies

Inner personal	Outer personal
Phenomenology	Empiricism
Existentialism	
Inner collective	**Outer collective**
Hermeneutics	Systems theory
	Marxism
	Capitalism

Figure 4

According to this view, the problems of Africa are caused by African philosophy ignoring or rejecting the "right hand".

The problems of the West are caused by Western philosophy ignoring or rejecting the "left hand".

If you are interested in finding out more about Ken Wilber, we recommend you consult the following: Wilber, K. 2001. *A Brief History of Everything*. Dublin: Gateway. You could also visit: www.integralinstitute.org., www.integralworld.net and en.wikipedia.org.

One word of warning: do **not** consult articles in the mainstream media about Ken Wilber and avoid discussions of his work by traditional Christians. Wilber has also been attacked by those working in the Western scientific establishment.

Credo Mutwa

Africa too, has its "system breakers". Credo Mutwa is a Zulu sanusi or shaman, and is the official storyteller and keeper of the Zulu people in South Africa. His knowledge has been made available to only the highest initiates of the African shaman tradition. Mutwa has pledged himself to expose what is really happening in the world and who is behind it. Here follows a poem he wrote committing himself to this end.

> When kings are slain, and a pope is sent to hell,
> when on a marble slab ... a murdered princess lies,
> a pale sacrifice to the beasts that rule the stars,
>
> When out of the sky a stricken warplane falls,
> trailing behind it long bridal veils of flame,
> as missiles rage and red hot cannon roar ...

Can we change our world?

When the battle tank briefly rules the blood drenched plains,
an iron tyrant on another's stolen throne ...
and its long cannon shatters the trembling skies with sound,

When nameless soldiers die friendless and unknown,
in Africa's valleys or Kosovo's snow-bound plains,
and whole tribes perish of hunger, disease and war ...

When money is built into a jail to hold humankind
and love has died and compassion is unknown ...
and lies become truth ... and truth becomes a lie in a nameless city,

When in streets who have no love,
numberless children know hunger and abuse ...
in countless homes where brute force rules supreme,

women have become blood-spattered slaves,
strangers to love, healing and respect,
strangers to the gentle and comforting word ...

Whose guilty shoulders must bear
the heavy beam of crucifixion, all the ill we see?
Whose quivering back must bear the barbed scourge?

For all the evil and all the pain we have known
weavers of lies, brewers of lies,
who can strike at people with weapons of the night

against which no armour and no shield can prevail.
The written word is their poison-coated sword,
the tinkling coin their cull and crop of maize ...

Murderers of nations, Africa's deadliest foes,
I curse your footsteps wherever you may go,
In whichever cave or dungheap you may hide,

I curse you all ... may Heaven blast your eyes,
Tell Jabulon, the demon you call God,
Nomabhunu's son defies him to his face,

I swear by the stones on my mother's sacred grave,
that as from this moment, I will fight you to the end.
Against your kind, against your Masters too,

I will not cease to raise the sword of Light.
For all you have done and all you have yet to do,
I will fight you to the end days ...

Other system beaters

The following are a few more ideas people have had about recreating our world and beating the system:

> There is no power that is exercised without a series of aims and objectives.
> (Michel Foucault, quoted in *Foucault for Beginners*)

> We have to deconstruct [take apart – *our explanation*] the foundations of international law, but not in order to destroy the international organisation. I think international organisations are something good, something perfectible, and something necessary, but we have to rethink the philosophical foundations of these international organisations.
> (Jacques Derrida, speaking at the Villanova University, USA, in 1994)

> Crayolas plus imagination – the ability to create images – these make for happiness if you're a child. Amazing things, Crayolas. Some petrol-based wax, some dye, a little binder – not much to them. Until you add the imagination. The Binney Company in Pennsylvania makes about two billion of these sticks of pleasure every year and exports them to every country in the United Nations. Crayolas are one of the few things the human race has in common ... Ronald Reagan and Gorbechev used crayons, I bet. So did Fidel Castro and the emperor of Japan and Gandhi and Mrs Thatcher and maybe even the Ayatollah ... Maybe we should develop a Crayola bomb as our next secret weapon. A happiness weapon. And every time a crisis developed, we would launch one. It would explode high in the air ... and then, when the Crayola bombs landed, people would smile and get a little funny look on their faces and cover the world with imagination ..."
> (Robert Fulghum, in *All I really need to know I learned in kindergarten*)

> The magic exists. (Steven King, in *It*)

> If I can construct cloth, I can construct my life. (Deborah Chandler, weaving teacher)

> Besides traditional objects of royal pleasure such as ceremonial knives, feathered fans and ornamental vases to hold precious oils, Tutankhamen's tomb contained some special mementos of the young King's childhood. Included among these were a toy-chest and a paintbox.
> (From *Ancient Egypt*, by Lional Casson, describing the tomb of Tutankhamen)

> And Jesus said to him, "Come, Zaccheus, make haste, for I must stay at your house today." So he made haste and came down and received Jesus joyfully. And when they saw it, they all murmured, saying "He has gone in to be the guest of a man who is a sinner." And Zaccheus stood and said to the Lord, "Behold, Lord, the half of my goods I give to the poor; and if I have defrauded any one of anything, I restore it fourfold." And Jesus said to him, "Today salvation has come to this house."
> (Christian Bible, New Testament, Gospel of Luke 19)

Can we change our world?

Once upon a time, in China, there lived two men: a wise man called Chitsu, and a wicked thief called Manan, whom everyone was afraid of. Chitsu was a true follower of Buddha: he lived poorly, spent many hours in meditation and was kind to all he met. One night, as he was meditating, the door of his hut burst open and the wicked thief, Manan, burst in, whirling his sword around and shouting "Where is your money? Give it to me now or I will kill you!!"

Chitsu opened his eyes and said: "All the money I have is in the pot on the shelf. You may take it, but please leave me two farthings so that I can pay my taxes tomorrow."

Manan glared at him, took all the money except the two farthings and, still brandishing his sword, made for the door.

"Excuse me," said Chitsu.

"What is it?" demanded Manan, rudely.

"You haven't said, 'thank you'," said Chitsu.

The next day, the villagers called on Chitsu. "We heard that Manan broke into your hut last night. Isn't he a horrible man?"

Chitsu looked surprised. "No, not at all. I found him quite a pleasant fellow. He even said thank you before he left me. He just needs to be a bit more careful with that sword of his, that's all."

(A Zen story)

I'd rather work 24 hours a day in my art studio and come in here and fall down on the bed than do anything else I know. Because this is living. It's like pure water, it's living. I've lived alone for years, and I've slowly cut out social life. I leave the world to the world.

(Louise Nevelson, artist, quoted in the preface to *The Path to the Beautiful*)

Critical theory in a nutshell

Critical theory claims that all human societies, particularly large and complex ones, are corrupted and distorted by deep-seated power structures. These power structures influence the way we live, the way we think and, indeed, the way we are.

Critical theory claims that our first task is to thoroughly understand what these power structures are and how they operate – we should then work to dismantle these structures.

If we ignore critical theory, we are likely to live our lives according to the whims and manipulations of these powerful structures. An example is a businessman who cannot imagine any other value system than that dictated by capitalism. As a result, he spends his entire life as a workaholic, anxiously wondering if he will ever make "enough" money. Another example is people who live entirely according to their cultural and kinship norms and who never stop to ask themselves, "But what do *I* want from life?"

six Rethinking a woman's world

In the 1950s, black South African women sang the following lyric while protesting against the apartheid pass laws:

> You have touched the women,
> You have struck a rock,
> You have dislodged a boulder,
> You will be crushed.

These words echo some of the sentiments expressed in many forms of feminism in the West and on the African continent, in the attempt on the part of women's movements to establish a "voice" for women in society.

Feminism

Feminism is a group of philosophies rather than one philosophy. Women from different cultures and different societies have designed their own forms of feminism. Today, we can list the following forms of feminism:

- African feminism (which deals with the whole question of Western colonisation, gender and white male domination in Africa)
- British and American feminism (divided into first- and second-wave feminism)
- European feminism (this tends to be more Marxist and/or existentialist than British and American feminism)
- Islamic feminism (which focuses on the place of women in Islam and generally contends that Islam gives moral and spiritual equality to men and women).

All forms of feminism, though, focus on the following issues:
- sexual stereotyping
- creating a bigger place for women in the world
- rejecting the view that women are inferior to men.

Rethinking a woman's world

Question

What does the word "feminism" mean to you?

Question

Can you remember where and when you first encountered feminism?

Question

What impact did it have on you?

Question

What roles do men and women play in your kinship network and domestic life?
   Are you happy with these roles, or do you think they need to be altered?

Question

What is your view of feminism? Do you think the world needs feminism?

> **Question:** If you are a man, what is your personal reaction to feminism?

The women's movement in Africa

In general, patriarchy is seen as being deeply embedded in the societal structures of the African continent, which contribute significantly to the oppression of African women. Yet there have been significant advances in the African women's movement, despite the fact that the continued destabilisation of the economy in Africa has marginalised women and invalidated their social institutions. Research in various parts of West Africa during the 1970s and 1980s, in South Africa during 1992, and in Liberia, Sierra Leone and Nigeria during 1994 indicates that women's groups focus on legal and social reform, violence against women, conflict resolution, economic empowerment and other issues in Africa. As a women's movement, African feminism can be described as a political, pragmatic, reflexive and group-orientated form of feminism, also referred to as "the sisterhood of Africa".

This form of a peculiarly African feminism focuses on the struggles of African women to create a space of independence and dignity out of a triple layer of oppression, namely, the oppressions created by colonial, Western patriarchal and African patriarchal cultures. Furthermore, it criticises Western and European feminists for trying to speak for African women, thus denying them the ability to voice their thoughts. African feminism argues that African liberation depends on the development of an independent feminist voice that will perpetuate the tradition of female involvement in African societal affairs. This critical response is directed at those attempts to interpret feminism as a Western cultural phenomenon, and which are seen to ignore alternative perspectives on feminism that emphasise the historical conditions under which women's movements, and particularly those in Africa, challenge patriarchal cultures.

African feminism also focuses on the politics of gender, that is, the power relations between men and women, which are structured around opposing notions of masculinity and femininity. In this regard, African women see their role as based on male-female complementarity in overcoming discrimination by means of more equitable gender relations and changes in the sexual division of labour in society.

South Africa has been described as a society in which patriarchy is deeply embedded, and women are oppressed by the social structure. However, since 1990, South Africa has been engaged in a process of fundamental reconstruction, and continues to strive for a non-racist, non-sexist society with the feminist movement contributing to this process.

Thought break

Question

To what extent has the feminist movement in South Africa been successful in bringing about an equitable gender dispensation in South African society?

Philosophers at work

Black women's studies in Africa, as a method of enquiry, has come to interpret feminism as a Western cultural phenomenon under whose influence local women's movements have challenged gender dimensions of customary laws in arguing for social change. In reaction to this form of colonisation, proponents of the women's movement in Africa have argued for the power of sisterhood that comes from recognising and respecting the multiplicity of perspectives that make up "feminisms" in Africa. Relying on post-colonial theory, they have explored issues such as the construction of the "other", and the unique perspectives and experiences of colonised races and cultures.

People who have been involved in black women's studies in Africa include the following:
- N'Dri Assie-Lumumba
- Florence Abena Dolphyne
- Amina Mama
- Lindiwe Zulu
- Maria Nzomo
- Mamphela Ramphele
- Catherine Odora Hoppers.
- Molara Ogundipe-Leslie
- Ifi Amadiume
- Nnaemeka Obioma
- Ama Ata Aidoo
- Philomina Okeke
- Rodo Barbre Gaidzanwa

The beginnings of American and British feminism

In the year 1848, in the town of Seneca Falls, New York, two women, Elizabeth Cady Stanton and Lucretia Mott, put their domestic duties aside for a while and sat down at a dining-room table to write the following words:

> We hold these truths to be self-evident: that all men and women are created equal ...
> The history of mankind is a history of repeated injuries and usurpations on the part of
> man toward woman, having the direct object of an absolute tyranny over her ... He has
> never permitted her to exercise her inalienable right to the effective franchise ... He has
> made her, if married, in the eye of the law, civilly dead ...

Like the men who drew up the American Declaration of Independence, some 200 years previously, these two women wanted a "better tomorrow".

How have men repeatedly injured women? This is not an easy question to answer, because women's experiences differ so enormously, depending on the country they live in, the religion that holds sway in that country, the social history of that country, etc. Also, women's experiences differ hugely even within one society. Some women, even in conservative, Islamic countries, can lead pleasant lives with access to education, literacy, mobility, social interaction and material wealth. Of course, their lives are restricted, but it is probably true to say that all human beings live with some degree of restriction.

So it is not easy to answer the question "How have men repeatedly injured women?" Some men clearly do not injure women, neither emotionally or physically, nor by supporting social injustice.

So what did Elizabeth Stanton and Lucretia Mott mean by the words "The history of mankind is a history of repeated injuries ... on the part of man toward woman"?

They meant several things. First of all, at the time they wrote, nowhere in the world did women have the vote. Politics and the affairs of the law and the state were run for men by men. Men passed laws, men voted for presidents, men determined who owned what. Women simply did not count. And the laws men passed included laws about divorce, marriage, child custody – areas of life that *determined the quality of women's daily lives*.

Property laws were a good example of the sort of laws men passed. A woman, when she married, became her husband's property. It was as simple as that. She did not exist as a person. If she had any possessions of her own, these became his. If the couple got divorced, he automatically got child custody. He could beat his wife without fear of legal reprisals. In short, a married woman was simply her husband's servant and prostitute.

Today, in most parts of the world, many men still do not treat women with kindness and compassion. Considering the following, written by the British writer and explorer Sir Ranulph Fiennes, when he was on a military operation in Oman in the late 1960s:

> An older woman suckled a baby opposite us; her exposed breast flat and wizened like
> her face. A single ring pierced her nose below cheeks livid with saffranin and tattooed
> with indigo streaks. Said bin Ghia saw me watching her. He chuckled, "She's in her early
> 20s, that one", he spoke in English, "it is the hard work that makes a woman old before
> her time."

The hard work and the ill treatment, I thought, for women are far from the first glimmers of emancipation in these parts. They can be bought whilst still sexually immature for a few cows or twelve dollars. The man who wants a girl need only gain the approval of her father or brother and must not already possess more than three wives. When he gets fed up with her he has but to visit the local judge and say the magic words – "I divorce three". The girl then has no one to support her and often no family to return to.

Despite this, they are happy enough and often sing sweetly as they work, their soft silver bracelets jangling and their faces usually free of the beaked mask of northern Oman. Their behaviour is loose and their main enjoyment is sex, made easier no doubt by their goat-grazing duties away from home. But the men get their own back brutally enough, for female babies are circumcised at the base of the clitoris to blunt their erotic nature. And fear of divorce makes many women place salt in their vaginas after childbirth to cause contraction and so please their husbands. All goes well till the next time a child is born and finds its exit blocked by vaginal scar tissue caused by the salt. Agony and death usually follow for the mother. Divorce would have been better.

Or consider this, taken from the *Weekly Mail and Guardian* (10 July, 2005) about the position of women living in the Punjab, India:

A Pakistani man and some of his relatives chopped off his wife's feet after accusing her of being promiscuous, police said on Saturday. The woman survived the gruesome attack, the latest in a wave of assaults that has raised international concern about the plight of women in rural Pakistan.

"It is a shameful act of cruelty against a woman," said Talat Ali, a senior police official in Punjab.

The 32-year-old woman told police her feet were chopped off on June 24 by her husband, her father-in-law, a brother-in-law and two others after they accused her of being "of bad character", a euphemism for promiscuous.

Violence against women is common in rural Pakistan where tribal and feudal customs hold sway. The latest incident occurred in central Punjab province, where the 2002 gang-rape of a woman, Mukhtaran Mai, on the orders of a village council, triggered an international outcry.

Pakistan President Pervez Musharraf, who is trying to project his country as a moderate Muslim nation, has condemned violence against women.

The woman in the latest incident had separated from her husband but had gone to his family's house to see her daughter, police said. Her father-in-law chained her up. That night, he and the others took her to the edge of their village and cut off her feet. Two days later, her parents reported her missing and police raided the house, found her and took her to hospital, where she remains.

"There is no evidence that she was of bad character," Ali said.

Guardian Unlimited © Guardian Newspapers Limited 2005

Rethinking our world

Question

Do these stories not suggest that men, in fact, hate women rather than love them?

Do you think that hate is based on fear?

Are men (or, at least, some men) deeply afraid of women?

Why should men fear women?

Why do men oppress women?

We are not sure, given that many patriarchal structures also oppress the vast majority of men. Also, in many parts of the world, including Africa, men discriminate against and pursue the oppression or exclusion of women in society as a result of religious and cultural beliefs which regard women as subordinate to men in the hierarchy of society and the community. As a result of these religious and cultural beliefs, men in our society are raised to fill public roles that are invested with real importance and significance, while women are expected to take the supporting roles of wives and mothers. This state of affairs appears to benefit men, who often derive status at the expense of their wives' labour and child-rearing positions. Also, and perhaps less obviously, we believe that all human beings are invested with certain survival instincts that make them seek, consciously and unconsciously, control over other people.

It may be that men – or, at least, large numbers of men – are dictated to by such instincts. It is also worth bearing in mind, we think, that a certain proportion of women gain from oppressive patriarchal arrangements. Think of the women married to dictators and those women who actively seek marriage to wealthy, powerful men. Flowing from this is the fact that one of the goals of the family is to raise children who have the same values as those of their parents and who will, therefore, pursue the same goals as their parents.

It is also alarming to note the resurgence of various forms of patriarchal world views in America. These patriarchal world views are associated, as the paragraph above suggests, with fundamentalist religious beliefs. The whole topic of the religious right in America, and the vulnerability of the American political system to the influence of extremist groups, is too huge to discuss in this chapter on feminism. What is important to note is that such groups have gained considerable power in America since 9/11 and are now a significant force in American politics.

For more information on the religious right in America we suggest you visit the following websites: www.theocracywatch.org and en.wikipedia.org.

Thought break

Why do you think men oppress women?

A brief history of women's rights movements in America and Britain

The history of women's rights owes much to the history of women's rights in these two first world countries.

America

1792: An English woman, Mary Wollstonecraft, publishes *Vindication of the Rights of Woman*, demanding that women be given equal political, social, education and civil rights. This book is the basis of both English and American women's rights movements.

1848: Elizabeth Cady Stanton and Lucretia Mott, two American women, draw up the Seneca Falls Declaration of Sentiments.

1851: The black woman and ex-slave Sojourner Truth gives her "Ain't I a woman?" speech at the women's rights convention in Ohio. Sojourner's powerful rhetoric (which was to be reflected, years later, in the speeches of Martin Luther King) ridiculed the notion that women were frail weaklings who needed men's protection.
1920: The Nineteenth Amendment guarantees American women the right to vote.

Britain

1869: John Stuart Mill publishes *The Subjection of Women*. In this book, Mill describes how boys and men are brought up to believe that women are their moral, spiritual and intellectual inferiors.
1903: The formation of the Women's Social and Political Union. Their newspaper, *Votes for Women*, sells 40 000 copies a week.
1914–1918: World War I. Women work in factories and mines, doing "men's jobs".
1918: Women over 30 win the right to vote.
1936: Vote given to all British women.

First-wave feminism

Despite the opposition of the Catholic Church, most women in Europe also gained the vote and various social rights during the first half of the 20th century. Today, women in some parts of Africa are gradually being integrated into formal institutions and social movements that create a new vision of gender relations in society.

The belief that women should be given the right to vote and that women should be equal before the law is known as "first-wave feminism". In the West, and in countries influenced by Western thinking (such as South Africa), this is the oldest form of feminism. Today, it is probably true to say that all educated men and women in the West at least accept the idea that women should be allowed to vote, own property, have divorce and child custody rights and be given access to birth control. Also, it is probably true to say that educated men and women believe that women should be given equal job opportunities and equal pay.

This type of feminism has links to the following methods of enquiry in philosophy:
- critical rationalism, which questions tradition
- critical theory, which challenges all forms of power
- empiricism, which asks us to look at reality objectively, including social reality.

If you are a Western woman, you could be tempted to take this form of feminism for granted, but in fact, many, many women in the world have *no rights whatsoever*. Indeed, in some countries, Islamic fundamentalism has taken away rights that women did have. Some examples are Afghanistan, Iran, Pakistan and some parts of Egypt.

Islamic fundamentalism is, in our opinion, rather a misleading phrase. A better description, we believe, would be "patriarchal fundamentalism". Patriarchal fundamentalism, as far as we can tell, is a system of fanaticism, usually spread and imposed on women *and many men* by a tiny handful of militarists who have gained recent political control of a society or country. Or, alternatively, it is a system that seems to be based on ageing despotic political dispensations and extreme poverty (in certain parts of India, for example). According to patriarchal fundamentalism, the Universe was created and is ruled by a male god who created men in his image to worship him. Everything else is non-divine and belongs to the class of animals, women included. By their very nature, such societies are not easy to explore or observe – but as far as we can tell, sexual relations in these societies consist of:

- highly regulated married sex between an older man and a very young woman, the sole purpose of which is to produce male children
- a high degree of prostitution, including child prostitution
- homosexual relations with young boys.

Feminist theology

Feminist theology began in earnest in the early 1970s, with the publication of Mary Daly's book, *Beyond God the Father: towards a philosophy of women's liberation*. Before this, in America, Britain and Europe, there had been increasing pressure on churches to give women more authority in the church.

Feminist theology asks one simple question: Who said God was male? The notion that God is male is, argue some feminist theologians, a direct violation of the First and Second Commandments:

> You shall have no other gods before me.
> You shall not make for yourself a graven image.

By insisting on the masculinity of God, say feminist theologians, we in fact worship maleness rather than the invisible and essentially unknowable God who is beyond any form of human understanding. In doing this, we have, in fact, made a graven image in our souls (and thus violated the Second Commandment).

What about the claim, in Christian theology, that Jesus referred to God as "Father"? Feminist theologians argue that there are a number of possible feminist responses to this question:

- Jesus himself was influenced by the patriarchal culture of his time.
- To describe God as Father is to use an analogy to depict God. It certainly does not mean that Jesus thought God was male.
- Feminists do not have to be threatened by calling God "Father", because this points to a redeemed masculinity.

> Feminist theologians point out that nowhere in the Gospels does Jesus once refer to women as being inferior to men.

At the beginning of the Christian Bible are the following words:

> The Lord God called to the man and said, "Where are you?" And the man said, "I heard the sound of you in the garden and I was afraid because I was naked and I hid myself." The Lord God said, "Who told you that you were naked? Have you eaten of the tree of which I commanded you not to eat?" The man said, "The woman whom thou gavest to be with me, she gave me fruit of the tree and I did eat." The Lord God turned to the woman. "What is this that you have done?" The woman said, "The serpent beguiled me, and I ate." … To the woman the Lord God said,
> "I will greatly multiply your pain in childbearing; in pain you shall bring forth children, yet your desire shall be for your husband, and he shall rule over you."

Thought break

Question

How much influence do you think this passage has had on women and on men's attitudes to women?

Philosophers at work

Feminism is the philosophy that claims the following:

1. Women are people in their own right.
2. Women should reject men's definitions of what makes a woman valuable.
3. Women should not make defensive claims to "equality with men". If anything, women are superior to men.
4. Women's happiness does not depend on having a romantic or marital relationship with a man. Women create their own happiness.
5. It is important that women do philosophy because philosophy, of all the academic disciplines, attempts to define and understand "reality". To date, virtually all philosophical work has been done by men and, as a result, people's understanding of "reality" is necessarily seriously distorted.
6. Only women have the right to pronounce on abortion because men do not get pregnant and bear children. Some feminists are pro-choice, others pro-life.

Feminism has links with the following methods of enquiry in philosophy:
- critical rationalism, because it questions the status quo
- critical theory, because it radically challenges the status quo
- African philosophy's attempts to "decolonise" the effects of domination by white males
- logical empiricism, because feminism precisely defines the problems women face
- empiricism, because it looks, scientifically, at the actual biological differences between men and women.

Feminism has given women enormous psychological and moral power, particularly women who have been "let down" by men (divorcees, single mothers, battered wives). Interestingly, this form of feminism is found outside the West – any group of women exchanging ideas, supporting each other is, in effect, practising this form of feminism.

People who have promoted feminism:
- Kate Millett (political philosopher)
- Germaine Greer (feminist theorist)
- Marilyn French (novelist and feminist theorist)
- Naomi Wolf (feminist theorist)
- Margaret Atwood (Canadian novelist)
- Betty Friedan (feminist theorist)
- Mary Daly (feminist theologian)

Activity

Try to get hold of and read one of the books on African feminism and one of the books on second-wave feminism listed in this chapter.
Do you see any similarities between African feminism and second-wave feminism?

Question

If you are a Muslim woman, what does feminism mean to you? A colleague of ours was informed by one of his male Muslim friends that the Qur'an and Mohammed preach women's equality. Do you agree?

Does it work?

What feminism can help us to do
1. Encourage women and men to re-examine their value systems.
2. Give women enormous psychological and moral power.
3. Help "rescue" traditional marriages that are failing.
4. Give women courage.
5. Bring alternative ideas to social problems.

Where feminism fails
1. It tends to dismiss the power and affection created by romantic love between men and women.
2. It limits dialogue and understanding between men and women.
3. It tends to portray all men as naturally predatory.
4. It encourages women to refuse to work alongside men – this may be self-defeating in terms of social change.
5. It tends to idealise women.

Activity

Now please read the following account, which is based on information contained in the online article "Project Independence" on the website of an organisation called Soroptimist International of Great Britain and Ireland.

From 2003 to 2007, Project Independence wants to help women who have been traumatised by male-led wars overcome their suffering and rebuild their lives and, if possible, the lives of some of the people around them. One of the ways of doing this is through microcredit lending. Microlending means sponsoring poor people – and the poorest people in the world today are women – by lending them small – very small – sums of money that will enable them to start modest but workable income-generating projects.

Interestingly, successful microcredit lending programmes operated today are based on the philosophies and policies of the Grameen Bank, set up by Muhammad Yunus, a Professor of Economics at the University of Chittagong in Bangladesh. 30 years ago, Professor Yunus came upon a virtually destitute woman in a village making bamboo stools. Professor Yunus simply couldn't understand why anyone who could make such beautiful things was so poor. The woman explained to Professor Yunus why she was so poor, despite the fact that she worked very hard and was a skilled worker. The root of her problem was that she had to borrow the money from men to whom she then had to sell the finished products. They paid her only a tiny sum for the stools she made, leaving her very little profit. Borrowing from a moneylender (again, all men) was out of the question because she would be charged 10% per day

Rethinking a woman's world

– 3 000% per year. She couldn't borrow from a bank because she had no collateral.

As Professor Yunus discovered, she was not the only woman in her village struggling to survive in the face of a male-dominated financial system that made certain men wealthy at the expense of the very poor. One of his first borrowers was a woman called Amina, a street beggar. Of her six children, four had already died of hunger. Immediately after she was widowed, Amina returned home to discover that her brother-in-law had turned her and her children out of "his" house. Muhammed Yunus' loan helped Amina start her own business making baskets. All that was needed to help such women was a mere $27! Professor Yunus told the women to pay the money back as and when they could. He got it all back and repeated the process in other villages. Thus the Grameen Bank Project was formed, microcredits being the new approach to lending money. The word Grameen means "rural" or "of the village".

Professor Yunus's vision, for the total eradication of poverty in the world using microcredit loans, was met with scepticism and hostility. Initially, his greatest opposition to lending poor women money came from husbands, who saw their position as "head of the household" as being under threat. Fortunately, Professor Yunus managed to win the men over. He even had answers for local Islamic community leaders who were against loans, as these are considered usurious. He told them that there was nothing in Shariah Law or the Koran against the project's work and that Grameen is owned by its borrowers, hence under Shariah Law, the ban on charging interest cannot apply.

Question

Of all the methods of enquiry in philosophy we have looked at so far, which one do you think is adopted by Muhammed Yunus?

Would you say he is a man who supports feminism?

Quick summary

Feminism is based on the principle that women have innate worth, inalienable rights, and valuable ideas and talents to contribute to society. Feminism goes beyond mere equality ... it insists not only that women be given equal rights to men, but that they be respected for themselves as well. At the heart of the women's rights movement has always been the idea that each individual has certain innate rights; that each individual is a valuable, contributing member of society.

In the description of the bad treatment of women in the Oman, Sir Ranulph Fiennes says:

> Despite this, they seem happy enough and often sing sweetly as they work, their silver bracelets softly jangling ...

Can his remarks give us a clue to the question we asked at the beginning of this book: What is happiness, anyway?

Feminism in a nutshell

Feminism claims that the entire experience of "being human" has been seriously damaged and distorted by masculine domination and the marginalisation of women.

Feminism claims that women have been, and are, denied basic human rights and that men have shown themselves to be unworthy leaders of the human race by repeatedly indulging in acts of war, violence and abusive power relationships.

If we ignore feminism, then it is likely that we will live in a state of barbarity rather than civilisation. This is because women, rather than men, bring stability, harmony and higher forms of culture (eg music, art) to human society. Societies that totally ignore the rights and needs of the female half of the human race tend to have enormous and intractable social problems. Examples of this at the time of writing are certain central African countries and countries in the grip of fanatical versions of Islam.

seven   Who in the world am I?

Some years ago, one of the authors of this book visited a Buddhist retreat just outside Johannesburg. The theme of the retreat that weekend was "Meditation for Westerners". The person in charge of the retreat and who took the participants through the meditation exercises, was a Buddhist monk, Rob Nairn. Like all the people attending the course, he was a Westerner brought up to believe in Western values (money, success, career). In his case, though, he had found that these values did not lead to happiness and joy, but to pain, disappointment and inner suffering. In his late twenties/early thirties, he had turned his attention away from his career (he had been a practising lawyer in Zimbabwe and, later, South Africa) and started studying the Buddhist scriptures.

When he was thirty-something, he gave up his career and entered a Buddhist monastery under a Tibetan teacher. He believed that this change would give him what he desperately needed: serenity and inner peace. He also believed that he would never attain serenity and inner peace unless he made peace with himself, with who he *really* was.

According to Buddhism and, in fact, all true religions, our greatest and most formidable encounter is not with the world, or the people we meet, or the external dangers we face, or the political system we live in.

Our biggest challenge is to come to terms with ourselves. Who are we when the "masks are off"? What are these masks that we wear every day? Who makes these masks and who, if anybody, forces us to wear them?

Activity

Go to the mirror and look at yourself. Can you look yourself straight in the eye? If you cannot, don't be surprised.

Society, and the people around us, makes many demands on us, right from the time we're young children. If, as children, we come into repeated contact with a person, people, or group of people who dominate us and force us into their way of doing things, it will be very difficult for us to discover "who we really are".

One of the things we've been looking at in this book is the experience of happiness.

One of the teachings of modern Buddhism is that we cannot be happy if we do not know who we are or if we have been taught to hate ourselves.

Stop and think for a moment.

Thought break

Can you think of any moment in your life when at that moment you experienced happiness and joy? What was that moment?

Activity

Let us not only look at the past. Turn to the present for a moment.
Put this book down. Sit still and comfortably, and pause.
What is happening in this moment, during this pause? What thoughts are going through your head? What are you experiencing in the world of your thoughts?

Finding time for reflection

Sitting quietly and doing some sort of inner exploration is, we believe, extremely important. It is something that our society actively discourages and it is something that certain groups of people rarely, perhaps never, have a chance to do. We are referring to people who work long hours in demanding jobs, who have large families and who, in short, are always seeking to meet the demands of others. Another thing that discourages this sort of inner seeking is constant noise and bustle.

Who in the world am I?

Thought break

Do you ever get time to do the sort of inner reflection we have referred to here?

If the answer is "no", why do you think this is?

Can you change the situation in any way?

The following is an extract from the writings of the late poet, Raymond Carver. As a writer, he desperately needed peace and quiet and time to reflect and write. His inability to find these things for many years drove him to despair and alcoholism. It was only when he was older, after he was divorced and his children had grown up, that he gained any sense of peace. We think that what Carver is saying here is highly significant.

> Up to that point in my life I'd gone along thinking, what exactly, I don't know, but that things would work out somehow – that everything I'd hoped for or wanted to do, was possible. But at that moment, in the laundromat that Saturday afternoon in Iowa City, I realized that this was simply not true. I realized – what had I been thinking before? – that my life was a small-change thing for the most part, chaotic, and without much light showing through ... At that moment – I swear this all took place in the laundromat ... I could see nothing ahead but years more of this kind of responsibility and perplexity. Things would change some, but they were never really going to get better. I understood this, but could I live with it? I'd had, I realized much later, an insight. But so what? What are insights? They don't help any. They just make things harder.
>
> Hard work, goals, good intentions, loyalty, my wife and I believed these were virtues and would someday be rewarded. We dreamt when we had the time for it. But, eventually, we realized that hard work and dreams were not enough. Somewhere, in Iowa City maybe, or shortly afterwards, in Sacramento, the dreams began to go bust.

Rethinking our world

The time came and went when everything my wife and I held sacred, or considered worthy of respect, every spiritual value, crumbled away.

(Raymond Carver, *Fires* [1985] pp. 33–34)

Question

What is your response to Carver's feelings? Have you ever felt like this?

Philosophers at work

The concern about what is going on inside us in relation to who we are, and how we as people relate to our world, is the focus of attention of that method of enquiry in philosophy referred to as phenomenology.

Because we are complicated, and the world is complicated, phenomenology is a complicated philosophy. It is also a very beautiful philosophy.

Unlike the other methods of enquiry in philosophy we have been looking at, phenomenology does not really contain "teaching". Nonetheless, it does have something to say to us. Phenomenology claims that human beings and the world interact with each other the whole time, the one influencing the other. It is possible to sum up phenomenology in the following statement:

"I am in the world and the world is in me."

Modern Western phenomenology is particularly concerned with the second part of this statement: "… the world is in me."

The modern world can be a deeply distressing and frightening place. Also, the modern world, for many Western people, centres increasingly on what is sometimes called "virtual reality". That is, the television, the computer screen, the video, the film. If the world that is in me is not real, then part of me will be unreal.

According to phenomenology, we need to connect with the real world.

The real world is the natural world of the Earth (trees, flowers, pets, mountains, the ocean) and other people (our spouse, children, the people in the street, everyone). The real world also includes things made by human beings: houses, tables and chairs, buildings, cars, highways, shops, clothes, ice cream, hamburgers, a glass of beer, a cup of coffee.

Other people are very important. Phenomenology believes that, if I am to be "real", then I need to have deep emotional connections with at least one other human being. But phenomenology also believes that we must be careful not to let other people "rule us" and drive us away from ourselves. We need to be careful, in fact, about the company we keep. One of the crucial points in phenomenology is that each and every one of us has a real, essential self with a vocation. (In the case of the late Raymond Carver, for example, this essential self needed to write or go mad with desperation.)

Phenomenology can be put into the following categories:
- Phenomenology of the self (who am I?)
- Social phenomenology (who and what is my community?)
- Cosmic phenomenology (our place in the Universe).

All these forms of phenomenology focus on the "real world". Phenomenology believes that the most dangerous thing is falsity. Falsity means to deceive, to mispresent, to distort. Falsity includes:
- individual pretence (an example is someone who is always out to impress everyone)
- social falsity (an example is a party where everyone tries to work out who is more important than whom).

Phenomenology asserts that we should not reduce people to things or objects by ignoring those huge areas of human experience that we can't "see" and "measure".

People who have promoted phenomenology:
- The Dalai Lama (Buddhist leader)
- Credo Mutwa (African shaman)
- Martin Heidegger (German philosopher)
- Jacques Derrida (French philosopher)
- Kwame Gyekye (African philosopher)
- Chuwudum Okolo (African philosopher)
- Oshita Oshita (African philosopher)
- Martin Luther King (Afro-American social activist)
- Albert Einstein (scientist)

Phenomenology and the mystery of human existence

Phenomenology is essentially concerned with what it is that makes us who we are as human beings. As a method of enquiry in philosophy, phenomenology encourages us to "wonder anew" at who we are, at who we long to be.

Thought break

> Suppose your doctor told you that you had only six months to live. What would you do during those six months? Would you continue to live your life as you are now?

At the beginning of his book *The Soul's Code*, the American psychologist James Hillman says this:

> We dull our lives by the way we imagine them. We have stopped imagining them with any sort of romance, any sort of story … [what about] beauty, mystery and myth?
> There is an essential mystery at the heart of each human life.

In this book, Hillman looks at the lives of people who have often rejected society's demands and said: "No. I must do this or die." Such people include the singer Ella Fitzgerald, the erotic dancer Josephine Baker, the violinist Yehudi Menuhin, the Spanish bullfighter Manolete.

Hillman writes as follows about the legendary filmmaker Ingmar Bergman. In this next extract Bergman is describing his yearning for a cinematograph (an early "movie machine"):

> More than anything else, I longed for a cinematograph. The year before, I had been to the cinema for the first time and seen a film … To me, it was the beginning. I was overcome with a fever that has never left me. The silent shadows turned their pale faces towards me and spoke in inaudible voices to my most secret feelings. Sixty years have gone by and nothing has changed; the fever is the same.

Question

> What is it that you long for? Do you know?

Who in the world am I?

Quick summary

Phenomenology looks at things and ourselves as they really are. Phenomenology believes that theories about ourselves and about life and the Universe can be very misleading and may lead to falsehood and deep unhappiness.

Historically, phenomenology has tended to promote religious belief because it asks us to look closely at our inner lives rather than our material possessions. Many of the world's great religious leaders practised phenomenology, including Buddha, Mohammed and, in the Christian tradition, St John of the Cross. However, in the late 20th and early 21st centuries, it is reasonable to say that science has moved closer to phenomenology in that science acknowledges the mystery of life and the mystery of the human person. Furthermore, none of the institutionalised religions that exist in the early 21st century, unfortunately, encourage inner exploration and reflection – if anything, they morally oppress and hector people into submission and conformity. If we want to find out who we really are, we are better off without these forms of religion.

Activity

Read the following, which is an excerpt from a public debate in 1999, between two scientists: Richard Dawkins (zoologist, Professor of the Public Understanding of Science at the University of Oxford and a well-known atheist) and Steven Pinker (neuroscientologist and Professor of Psychology at Harvard University, also an atheist). Dawkins is speaking:

> Carl Sagan, an American astronomer–author, wrote, shortly before he died, "How is it that hardly any major religion has looked at science and concluded, 'This is better than we thought! The Universe is much bigger than our prophets said, grander, more subtle, more elegant'? Instead they say, 'No, no, no! My god is a little god, and I want him to stay that way.' A religion, old or new, that stressed the magnificence of the Universe as revealed by modern science might be able to draw forth reserves of reverence and awe hardly tapped by the conventional faiths."
>
> Well it's common enough for people to agree that religions have got the facts all wrong, but "Nevertheless," they go on to say, "you have to admit that religions do provide something that people need. We crave a deeper meaning to life, a deeper, more imaginative understanding of the mystery of existence." Well, in the passage I've just quoted, Sagan seems to be criticizing religions not just for getting it wrong, which many people would accept, but for their deficiencies precisely in the sphere in which they are supposed to retain some residual virtue. Religions are not imaginative, not poetic, not soulful. On the contrary, they are parochial, small-minded, niggardly with the human imagination, precisely where science is generous.

> Now, there are, of course many unsolved problems, and scientists are the first to admit this. There are aspects of human subjective consciousness that are deeply mysterious. Neither Steve Pinker nor I can explain human subjective consciousness – what philosophers call qualia. In *How the Mind Works* Steve elegantly sets out the problem of subjective consciousness, and asks where it comes from and what's the explanation. Then he's honest enough to say, "Beats the heck out of me." That is an honest thing to say, and I echo it. We don't know. We don't understand it.
>
> What is your response to Professor Dawkins's remarks about religion? Do you agree with him?
>
> _____
>
> _____
>
> What is your response to his remarks about human subjective consciousness?
>
> _____
>
> _____
>
> Our response
>
> We personally feel that Professor Dawkins is right. It is possible to find and create meaning without conventional forms of religion. We also personally feel it is possible to acknowledge life's mystery, and the mystery of human identity – what Dawkins calls "human subjective consciousness", without conventional forms of religion. Perhaps you disagree.

The problem of identity

Who we are is connected to our personal past, our culture, our parents, our upbringing and our life today. We know what our life is today, but how do we go back into the past?

Think about your parents and grandparents – how much do you know about them? How much can you remember about your childhood?

Much of our past is lost and forgotten. Even if we grow up in a home where the past is treated with great respect, where there are photo albums of us from when we were small children to the present, there will always be huge gaps. In many homes, of course, the past is remembered through stories. And, tragically, many people grow up in circumstances that are distressing (eg broken homes, families separated because of apartheid, extreme poverty).

It is actually very difficult to answer the question: "How did we come to be as we are?"

It is even more difficult to answer the question, "Who are we?"

Religious leaders and the self

Buddha – Gautama Buddha, more than any other major religious leader, emphasised human beings' need to discover their true self. Buddha himself was born into a wealthy family and was destined to take over the social role and privileges of a young nobleman. This was not to be. His confrontation with suffering, death and the realisation that human life is short forced him to become a wandering ascetic. After some years of this, he found his own path – "The Middle Way". This Way, he claimed, would lead all human beings to enlightenment about their inner being, primarily through meditation – which is aimed at freeing the mind of delusion and falsity. Although the religion of Buddhism has not been without its low points, Buddhism has, on the whole, not imposed itself on society in the way that Islam and Christianity have.

Jesus of Nazareth – A reading of the four gospels of the Christian Bible makes it clear that Jesus's way was quite different from Buddha's. Jesus himself was convinced that our first duty is to love God with all our heart, mind and soul. It is important to realise, however, that this is not to negate the self – far from it. By loving God, we will come to experience deep spiritual fulfilment. Jesus's message was spelt out by St Augustine: "We are made in Your Image, O God, and our hearts can find no rest until we reside in Thee." Christianity at the beginning of the third millennium means rediscovering, and re-emphasising, contemplative prayer and our need for inner healing. There is increasing dialogue between Christians and Buddhists. Some Christians today are extremely critical of the monolithic structures of the churches and the way certain churches have been, and still are, prepared to dominate human beings and, in effect, run people's lives for them.

Mohammed – A sentence in the Qur'an reads "God is closer to man than his jugular vein". Mohammed himself believed he had had a direct experience of the divine and this belief passed into Islamic mysticism (called Sufism). Muslims, and particularly those who consciously follow a mystical path, believe that certain forms of prayer, movement and even dance bring human beings into the presence of Allah. As in Christian mysticism, Islamic mysticism often portrays Allah as human beings' "lover" and "friend" – the One God all of us need if we are to find our powers of self-expression, creativity and inner serenity. The history of the religion of Islam, unfortunately, like the history of Christianity, has been marked by militarism, violence and, in some countries, the horrific treatment of women. In recent years, criticisms of institutionalised, highly conservative forms of Islam have been numerous and have arisen from both within and outside Islam and from women and men. For example, the first international congress on feminism and Islam (organised by a Muslim man, Mr Prado), was held in Spain at the end of October 2005. This congress was peaceful and characterised by calls to rethink traditional "male chauvinist" interpretations of certain passages in the Qu'uran.

The Ancient Egyptians and the problem of cultural identity

One of the most puzzling and mysterious of all past African cultures is Ancient Egypt. Ancient Egypt is Egypt from 2181 BC until 1069 BC. In other words, Ancient Egypt existed for over 1 000 years.

The Ancient Egyptians left behind huge amounts of information about themselves. They wrote, painted and had very complex burials for their kings and queens.

Historians know, or think they know, that the Egyptians had very strong religious beliefs and convictions about the afterlife. The Ancient Egyptians believed that all human beings had a soul that would be judged by the gods after death. In Egyptian tombs, the soul is drawn as a small angel figure that hovers over the dead body before leaving it.

And yet, if the soul was so important, why did the Egyptians mummify their dead? Why were they so anxious to prevent the dead from decaying for as long as possible? Why did they put these bodies in huge pyramids? Medical experts have been able to take blood samples from some of these bodies and have tried, with limited success, to identify (via DNA) relationships between the different kings and queens.

Despite their writings and paintings, no historian has ever succeeded in achieving a final interpretation of the vast symbolism that the Egyptians left behind. The Egyptians talk about the time the gods "walked among them". What gods? What memories are they talking of? What myths?

The most startling of all discoveries in the 20th century was the tomb of Tutankhamen. The tomb was discovered and opened by the Englishman, Howard Carter, in 1922. According to the history books, Tutankhamen was a very unimportant, insignificant young king. But we believe he was significant, although we don't know why and, possibly, we never shall.

Why do we believe he was not insignificant? Because of the love, care and valuable treasure with which he was buried. Somebody, somewhere, for some reason, believed in this young king so much so that they put a beautiful mask over his face and erected a lovely statue of the goddess Serket to guard the vessel that contained his innermost organs. The people who buried him made sure that, when he awoke from his sleep of death, Tutankhamen would find a boat that would carry him away to a far country.

They even left him a wishing-cup, on which was written the following:

Mayest thou spend millions of years, thou lover of Thebes, sitting with thy face to the North wind and thy eyes beholding felicity.

"Felicity" means "happiness".

Does it work?

What phenomenology can help us to do
1. Examine our lives closely.
2. Reject false value systems (eg materialism).
3. Slow down and lead less stressful lives.
4. Resist other people's demands and expectations.
5. Find happiness.

Where phenomenology fails
1. It can accept social evil.
2. It leads to mental confusion.
3. It can be very morally demanding.
4. It has been criticised for not being a problem-solving philosophy.
5. It tends to be too uncritical of authority.

Some examples of phenomenology

In seeking to come to terms with existential realities, and in an effort to understand the universe, African cultures draw on explanatory models that may appear at variance with perceptual experience ... We can say that the African realises the enormous complexity of the universe, and is aware that mankind and its world constitute an 'environment' much deeper than the human senses can perceive. The essence of African metaphysics, then, is the search for meaning and ultimate reality in the complex relationship between the human person and his/her total environment.

(Lesiba J Teffo & A P J le Roux, in *Philosophy from Africa*)

As a Buddhist I have found that one's own mental attitude is the most influential factor in becoming a happy person. In order to change conditions outside ourselves, we must first change within ourselves. Inner peace is the key.   (The Dalai Lama)

They are all gone now. My brother, my father, even my wife Jessica has died. Only I am left, and still I sat here at the river. I am haunted by water ... this country of mountains, trees and sky, and a river running through it.

(From the film *A River Runs Through it*, directed by Robert Redford)

Rethinking our world

The fairest thing we can experience is the mysterious. It is the fundamental emotion which stands at the cradle of true art and true science. A knowledge of the existence of something we cannot penetrate, of the manifestation of the profoundest reasons and the most radiant beauty, which are only accessible to reason in their most elementary forms – it is this knowledge and this emotion that constitute the truly religious attitude; in this sense, and this sense alone. I am a deeply religious man. (Albert Einstein)

Nature must be freely at work in the mind when anything is well made.
(From *The Unknown Craftsman* by Soetsu Yanagi, quoted in *The Craft of Handspinning*, by Eileen Chadwick)

The journey of discovery has taken me to new territories, territories from which the place of *Homo sapiens* in the universe of things is more clearly perceived.
(Richard Leakey, anthropologist)

In that moment I knew that to play the violin was to be. (Yehudi Menuhin)

Question What does all this say to us?

Question How do we respond?

Question What is in your "wishing cup"?

Phenomenology in a nutshell

Phenomenology asks: "Who am I?" Who is this "I" that constantly interacts with the world around me?

Phenomenology claims that our biggest challenge is to confront ourselves in all our ambiguity and complexity and thus to get nearer to the "real me".

Phenomenology encourages us to resist power structures by a process of retreat and non-engagement rather than confrontation.

If we ignore phenomenology, we run much the same risks as when we ignore existentialism. We will probably lack the capacity to "feel" and we are likely to never, or rarely, experience moments of real joy or real pain. A society that ignores phenomenology runs all the same risks as a society that ignores existentialism.

eight   Is there a world that speaks to us?

The well-known anthropologist (anthropology is the study of humans, their origins, their societies, religions, institutions and customs), Richard Leakey, says the following in his book *Origins Reconsidered*:

> In many ways it is language that makes us feel human. Ours is a world of words. Our thoughts, our world of imagination, our communication, our rich culture – all these things are woven on the loom of language. Language can conjure up images in our minds. Language can stir our emotions – sadness, happiness, love, hatred. Through language we can express individuality or demand group loyalty. Quite simply, language is our medium.

Question

Do you agree with Richard Leakey? Or do you think human beings express themselves in other ways too?

We are not certain that we completely agree with Richard Leakey here. After we read those words, we wrote down a list of all the things we could do to communicate without using language.

This is what we came up with:
- play music
- paint and draw
- scream
- cry
- smile

Is there a world tht speaks to us?

- frown
- dance
- make things (for example, pottery and sewing).

> **Question**
> Can you think of anything else?

The symbols of the Universe

The British physicist Stephen Hawking suffers from a disease known as Lou Gehrig's disease. This disease attacks the central nervous system and leaves the victim more and more helpless as time goes by. Today, Stephen Hawking has to speak, laboriously, through a special computerised voice synthesiser. Even then, it is difficult for journalists and students to understand what he is saying.

Fortunately for Hawking, he works in the field of mathematics and it is through mathematical symbolisation and proofs that he has managed to communicate his ideas about space and time. *Time* magazine described Hawking's work as follows:

> While still a graduate student, he became fascinated by black holes, the bizarre objects created during the death throes of large stars. Working with mathematician Roger Penrose, he developed new techniques to prove mathematically that at the heart of black holes were singularities – infinitely dense, dimensionless points with irresistible gravity – and he went on to calculate that the entire universe could have sprung from a singularity ... the Big Bang. In the hot big bang model the rate of expansion is always decreasing with time, but in the inflationary model the rate of expansion increases rapidly in the early stages." (Stephen Hawking, in *A Brief History of Time*)

Albert Einstein

You don't have to be a physicist to know the set of symbols for Einstein's formula for relativity: $E = mc^2$.

You probably know what these letters stand for, but in case you've forgotten:
   E means energy
   m means mass
   c means speed of light

Modern mathematics is extremely difficult to understand for most of us, so it is a relief to know that more and more physicists are starting to get away from mathematical symbolism and are using pictures instead, which are less threatening.

In fact, one of the things that is happening now is that scientists are starting to ask, "What shape is the Universe?"

They've come up with the following:

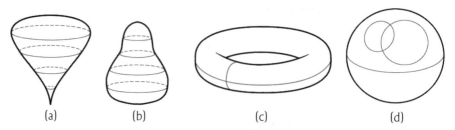

Figure 5: Shapes of the Universe

Which one do you feel happiest with? We rather like b above.

Charlene Bate, who did the layout for this book, drew this shape to describe her Universe:

Figure 6: Another Universe

Question

What does your idea of the Universe look like?

Wassily Kandinsky

Above, we said that modern mathematics was a bit threatening to most of us. This is probably because mathematics is so difficult to understand. So it's heartening to know that mathematics can be turned into other languages. We saw how this worked when we looked at the shapes of the universe.

Arts and maths tend to be "enemies" – many people who are good at art hate maths and people who are good at maths often feel that art is a waste of time. But an artist who wanted to bring the two together asked rather odd questions:

> Do numbers have colours? Do geometric shapes have colours?

This artist was Wassily Kandinsky. The details of Kandinsky's life do not really matter here. What is important is that Kandinsky did his major artistic work on colours and numbers about five years after Einstein's Theory of Relativity had been accepted as the most accurate view of the Universe. The symbols of mathematics, line and form were suddenly the most important thing human beings possessed – or so it appeared at the time.

In 1926, Kandinsky made the following statement:

> The hot and cold character of the square, with its obviously flat nature, makes one think of red, an intermediary colour between yellow and blue, which itself possesses this hot-cold quality ... Among all the angles, one must choose a certain angle situated between the right angle and the acute angle; an angle of 60 degrees ... when these angles are jointed by their openings, one has an equilateral triangle and one thinks of yellow. Thus, the acute angle is yellow. The obtuse angle gradually loses its aggressiveness, its heat, and thus it vaguely evokes a non-angular line, which constitutes the primary surface: the circle ... this needs a slight blue tinge.

Visit the following website to look at some of Kandinsky's work: http://www.ibiblio.org/wm/paint/auth/kandinsky/.

> Few cross the river of time and reach Nirvana. Most of us run up and down only on this side of the river. But those who when they know the law follow the path of the law, they shall reach the other shore.
> (Buddhist teaching)

Mandala

A Buddist mandala is a diagram used as a focus and guide for meditation. Each mandala represents the universe pictorially. Create your own wish list and then decide what colours to paint each wish. If you've got children, or you work with children, why not get them involved?

Figure 7: Buddhist Mandala

Question

What is the colour of your Universe, your world?

_____

_____

Activity

Look at our wish list in Chapter 3. We said we wanted to grow exotic roses and own a penthouse flat and travel the world, and …

What colour do you think the authors' Universe is? Is it many colours?

_____

_____

Other symbols

Not everyone likes mathematics and not everyone likes art. Some people like music – they play a musical instrument and/or they have a nice singing voice.

If music speaks to you, you will probably understand this:

None of these signs and symbols speaks to the authors of this book. We like listening to music, but we cannot sing and we have not learnt to play a musical instrument.

Is there a world that speaks to us?

But the following signs and symbols do speak to Jane because she has a loom and is interested in weaving:

These symbols are weaving symbols. They tell weavers how to operate a loom to get certain patterns. These particular symbols tell the weaver how to weave a pattern called "a thousand flowers". This pattern has many, many different possibilities. It was originally a pattern used by Finnish weavers, and was taken from Finland to Minnesota, USA, in the very early part of the 20th century. One of its most beautiful possibilities is shown above. Strangely, weaving is sometimes practised by blind people who use their fingers and hands to "feel" the pattern they are weaving.

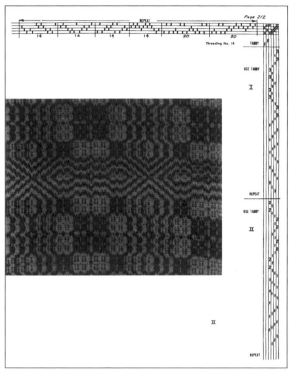

Figure 8: The "thousand flowers" pattern

Thought break

What else speaks to people, do you think?

The following is an extract from a book on religion in South Africa, describing symbols used by San Bushmen in their rock art.

> Southern African rock art displays enormous diversity and variability in age, place and content. After all, we are dealing with a timespan of roughly 25 000 years, and a geographical area the size of Europe. I wish to draw attention to the recurring motif of

Rethinking our world

the circle/spiral in Bushman engravings, interpreting it as expressive of Bushman religion, but not just religion. These figures express and evoke associations of beauty, truth and openness for those of us who live on the edge of Western-Christian power. The perspective I am presenting makes no claim to correspond with an objectively present Bushman world; also I make no attempt to escape from the spiral of understanding, I shuttle backwards and forwards between my own presuppositions and the world of the Bushmen ... As can be seen at Driekopseiland, circles occur in various forms: simple circles; circles containing crosses, emanating rays; concentric circles; or open-ended spirals ... It is not possible, or necessary, to "prove" what these Bushmen artists intended. We no longer have access to the minds of the artists ... Circles and spirals are universal expressions of a profound religious intuition. They arise from the deeper level of human consciousness, which is a storehouse of powerful symbols. (J S Kruger, in *Along Edges*)

Kruger speaks of truth, beauty and "openness". He obviously likes circles.

Question — What about you? What shapes speak to you of truth, beauty and openness?

Kruger also says that he "make(s) no attempt to escape from the spiral of understanding, I shuttle backwards and forwards between my own presuppositions [that is, opinions] and the world of the Bushmen".

Here are some of the shapes found in Bushman (San) art:

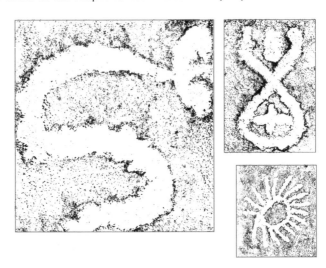

Figure 9: San symbols

> **Activity**
>
> Look through some consumer magazines and see if you can spot any similarities between the shapes we've been looking at in this chapter and the pictures in the magazines. Look for circles, faces, criss-crossed lines. What are the most common colours?
>
> If you have children, or you work with them, some of them might be interested in doing this with you.
>
> Look at the pictures in the magazines and then re-read what Kruger says about San art.
>
> Did any of the pictures from the magazines speak to you of truth, beauty and openness?

Philosophers at work

The method of enquiry in philosophy that focuses on symbols and how we interpret them is called hermeneutics. The word "hermeneutics" comes from a Greek word meaning "interpretation".

Hermeneutics is very similar to another method of enquiry in philosophy that we looked at, existentialism. This is because existentialism asks, "What is the meaning of life?" Hermeneutics asks, "How do we discover or create meaning?" In other words, how do we understand and interpret the different kinds of symbols we encounter in our world?

The following are some of the main ideas that are propagated by hermeneutics:

- hermeneutics emphasises the importance of listening and observing
- hermeneutics claims that the individual's life-experience influences the way he or she understands the world
- hermeneutics affirms the importance of dialogue in arriving at an understanding of any issue
- hermeneutics is anti-authoritarian and encourages the individual to create his or her own meaning and understanding.

Today, unfortunately, hermeneutics has been ignored owing to the huge impact of science, technology and consumerism.

Rethinking our world

> The joke is, though, that consumerism and advertising often talk about "the symbols of success". You know what these symbols are: cellphones, a BMW car, designer clothes and a smart house or flat. If you want to get the feel for some of these symbols and how they work, a good place to visit is Vodaworld, just outside Midrand, Johannesburg. An upmarket shopping mall is also full of these symbols.
>
> People who have promoted hermeneutics:
> - Carl Jung (Swiss psychologist)
> - Hans-Georg Gadamer (German philosopher)
> - Martin Heidegger (German philosopher)
> - Wilhelm Dilthey (philosopher)
> - Tsenay Serequeberhan (African philosopher)
> - John Mbiti (African philosopher)
> - Ngugi wa Thiong'o (African writer)
> - Cain Hope Felder (Afro-American New Testament scholar)

Carl Jung

The best known of the people who have promoted hermeneutics is probably Carl Jung. He was a psychologist who believed that all human beings interpret their world, their lives and themselves in certain ways. Jung claimed that our universe contains what he called "universal symbols". These symbols, said Jung, are the key to our healing and happiness and give us clues about how we should live our lives. Carl Jung lived from 1875 to 1961. He wrote several books for people who did not have training in psychology. These are: *Memories, Dreams, Reflections* and *Man and his Symbols*. Jung claimed that these universal symbols often come to us in our dreams and fantasies. If we ignore them, or if the society we live in does not allow us access to these symbols, then illness and unhappiness will be the result.

Jung identified a number of universal symbols: the mandala, the phallus, the Mother, the Father, the moon, the sun, the key, the circle and the cross. Here, Jung comments on how we can interpret our dreams and nightmares.

> PATIENT: "Yes, I have terrible dreams. Only recently I dreamt I was coming home at night. Everything is as quiet as death. The door into the living room is half open, and I see my mother hanging from the ceiling, swinging to and fro in the cold wind that blows through the open windows. Another time I dreamt that a terrible noise broke out in the house at night. I get up and discover that a frightened horse is tearing through the rooms. At last it finds the door into the hall, and jumps through the hall window from the fourth floor onto the street below. I was terrified when I saw it lying there, all mangled.

JUNG'S INTERPRETATION: We need to look more closely into the meaning of the two main symbols, "mother" and "horse". These symbols must be identical, because they both commit suicide. "Mother" ... refers to the place of origin, to nature, to that which passively creates ... the hollow form, the vessel that carries and nourishes ... the unconscious life ... [the dream tells us that] the patient's unconscious life is destroying itself. Horse ... stands for the animal life of the body ... so the animal life is also destroying itself ... the dream speaks a language.

(From *Selected writings*, edited by Storr)

Just supposing ...

Just suppose you were killed in a road accident today ...

Question

What would your possessions say about you? Do you own many things, or only a few things? What network of human relationships are you involved in? What would these relationships say about you?

Who is the person closest to you?

Which possession do you prize the most?

Quick summary

The method of enquiry in philosophy that examines symbols and the meaning of symbols is called hermeneutics.

People who practise this method of enquiry in philosophy consciously ask themselves: "What creates and produces meaning? Can human beings live without meaning? Is there a link between despair, violence and meaninglessness?

This method of enquiry in philosophy tends to focus on literature, art, film, poetry, music and craft. Today, it increasingly confronts science and demands that scientists give us meaningful science rather than "cold, objective" science.

Does it work?

What hermeneutics can help us to do
1. Create meaning.
2. Discover our own hidden artistic abilities.
3. Resist scientific arrogance and domination.
4. Understand each other.
5. Be more tolerant of each other.

What hermeneutics can't help us with
1. Define problems.
2. Overcome injustice.
3. Be decisive.
4. Take action.
5. Be more logical.

Symbols – light in the dark?

The popular writer of horror stories, Stephen King, is quoted as saying the following, in an interview in early 1999:

> Sometimes at night I'll see a pattern of shadows and I'll be convinced it tells me about the later stages of existence. Or there's the textured quality of dreams. What other worlds do they come from?

Question

When you think of darkness, what symbols and "pattern[s] of shadows" come to your mind?

What symbols do you associate with death and destruction?

Is Stephen King talking about death here? Or about something else?

Is there a world that speaks to us?

We feel that he is referring not to death, but to potential – to future possibilities. We say this because of the way he links patterns with dreams. It is in darkness that we have our dreams. It is in darkness that we reflect, if we reflect at all, on ourselves, our worlds, our futures, our pasts. It is in darkness that we remember.

Activity

Read the following, written by the German philosopher, Georg Hegel:

> This descent into dark regions where nothing reveals itself to be fixed, definite and certain, where glimmerings of light flash everywhere but, flanked by abysses, are rather darkened in their brightness and led astray by the environment, casting false reflections far more than illumination. Each beginning of every path breaks off again and runs into the indefinite, loses itself, and wrests us away from our purpose and direction. From my own experience I know this mood of the soul, or rather of reason, which arises when it has finally made its way with interest and hunches into a chaos of appearance and, though inwardly sure of the goal, has not yet worked through them to clarity …"
>
> (Hegel, quoted in *Hegel for Beginners*)

What do you think Hegel is talking about here? What is he struggling with?

Have you ever had this sort of experience? What happened to you?

What caused it, do you think?

Does the past contain good memories for you or is the past a source of pain?

Jean Baudrillard and signs

Jean Baudrillard is a French philosopher who has looked closely at the symbols of consumer society. Baudrillard's approach to the philosophy of meaning is a very Western approach – basically, he was fascinated by two things: the shopping mall and Disneyland.

Baudrillard asked a simple question "What is a shopping mall? What happens in shopping malls?"

He came up with the following answer: The shopping mall is the place where we *identify* with the things we buy. We even have a sort of identity with the things we don't buy.

What did Baudrillard mean by this?

Let's take the example of a wristwatch. Suppose I want to buy a new wristwatch. Which brand am I going to buy?

That will depend, essentially, on two things: how much I can afford to pay for a watch and the kind of watch I want to wear.

Suppose I have only a small amount of money. In this case, I will buy a cheap watch from, say, Clicks. But the problem I have now, according to Baudrillard, is that wearing this watch says, "I'm poor and therefore insignificant." So what do I do?

Maybe I don't mention my watch to anybody. Or, maybe, if someone notices my new watch, I say something like: "Yes, I just bought this cheap watch – I'm a practical sort of person – I didn't want one of those fancy things – I just need something that tells the time."

In other words, the watch has forced me to define myself within the consumerist system.

The worst of it, said Baudrillard, is that this isn't just true of something like a wristwatch. Consumerism has invaded the whole of life. Consumer symbols are so powerful that they define us.

Worse still, these symbols are often little more than plastic rubbish:

> Consumption diminishes the human species, but how can we challenge the satisfaction of someone who buys a pedal bin covered with flowers?

If you think all this is an exaggeration, go to a shopping mall during the working week and have a good look at what is going on around you.

Ken Wilber and meaning

> Because the universe has direction, we ourselves have direction. There is meaning in the movement, intrinsic value in the embrace [of the Kosmos]... we lie in the lap of immense intelligence, which by any other name is Spirit. There is a theme inscribed on the original face of the Kosmos. There is a pattern written on the wall of Nothingness.

There is a meaning in its every gesture, a grace in its every glance. We – and all beings – are drenched in this meaning, afloat in a current of care and profound value, ultimate significance, intrinsic awareness. We are part and parcel of this immense intelligence, this Spirit-in-action, this God-in-the-making ...
(Wilber 2001:38)

Steve Biko speaks

In rejecting Western values, therefore, we Africans are rejecting those things that are not only foreign to us but that seek to destroy the most cherished of our beliefs – that the corner stone of society is man himself – not just his welfare, not his material wellbeing, but just man himself ... We reject the power-based society of the Westerner that seems to be ever concerned with perfecting their technological know-how while losing our on their spiritual dimension. We believe that in the long run the special contribution to the world by Africa will be in this field of human relationships. The great powers of the world may have done wonders in giving the world an industrial and military look, but the great gift still has to come from Africa – giving the world a more human face.
(Biko quoted in *The Essential Steve Biko*)

Hermeneutics in a nutshell

Hermeneutics takes imagery and symbolism seriously. Hermeneutics claims that arts and crafts, even more than science, are important in human life.

Hermeneutics believes that happiness is linked with our own creativity in whatever form that takes, and in whatever cultural context it is produced.

Hermeneutics encourages us to be poets, writers, authors, actors, painters, musicians, weavers, potters, quilt-makers, gardeners, cooks, homemakers and designers. It does not disparage science and technology, but believes that this is only part of human achievement.

If we ignore hermeneutics, then we will be deeply unhappy people because we will be ignoring our needs as human beings. Unfortunately, there is a very real risk that this may be happening to children brought up in Western schooling systems. In the digital race, the focus is increasingly on pressurising children and young people to "perform" in mathematics, science and computer technology, while ignoring human and cultural studies.

nine Where in the world are we going?

At the beginning of this book, we made a number of statements about philosophy. One of them was:

> [Philosophy does not give] us a simple creed to follow or a message of comfort in the life to come, but [it] has the power to emancipate us in a strange, magical and oddly sacred way.

And it does this in a way that is disarmingly simple: it invites us to question *everything we have ever been told and ever believed.*

All the methods of enquiry followed by philosophy that we have looked at in this book do this.

One method of enquiry that pursues the questioning process to what some believe to be an extreme, is known as *postmodernism*. To understand postmodernism, we need to know what "modernism" is.

Modernism

Modernism is the belief that has dominated Western society, and therefore most of the world, for the last two centuries or so.

> Modernism: science, reason and technology will fix it all

It is not easy to define modernism. But we can say that it is based on the conviction that science has improved, and will improve, the lives of human beings. Science has enabled us to cure many diseases; it has enabled us to make our farming methods more efficient and it has given us the technological, urban world of today: digital gadgets, hospitals, schools, computers, cars, satellite television, and so on.

Modernism was probably at its strongest during the years following World War II, in the late 1940s and 1950s. At the time, in the West, slums were destroyed, children were innoculated against the old killer diseases of the past: polio, smallpox, TB. Money was poured into new education systems. Western economies boomed and unemployment was minimal. The motor car, telephone and television became part of virtually everyone's lives. By the early 1960s, the average Westerner fully believed that the future held little to fear. Soon, even poor countries such as Africa and India would benefit from scientific achievement and they too would enjoy material plenty or, at least, would see visible improvement in the lives of most of their people.

There is another side to modernism, too.

Modernism believes that the ideal human being is a cool, calm, rational person who can be relied upon to solve problems. Modernism believes that the ideal world will be a world ruled by reason and technology. Of course, modernism accepts that we all have emotions and have personal relationships, but it believes that emotions and relationships need to be "watched". This is where psychology comes in, the "science of the human person". If I find myself getting involved with love affairs that go wrong, or I find myself constantly quarelling with the people I work with, then I should go to a psychologist to find out what's wrong. Then I will be a perfectly balanced person, well able to take my place within a highly technological society.

Until very recently, most Westerners accepted this view of life and themselves unquestioningly.

But some time during the late 1960s and on into the 1970s, all this confidence simply evaporated.

Science was not keeping its promises. Western society became bedevilled by certain social problems: growing violent crime, huge increases in unemployment, a widening rich-poor gap, urban riots, racial unrest in British and American cities, political extremism.

Even medical science was starting to look suspect. Certain forms of cancer could still not be cured. Aids came along. Greater numbers of people were dying of heart disease. Mental illness was widespread: depression, anxiety, substance-dependency.

This is where postmodernism comes in.

> Postmodernism: science, reason and technology could not fix it all. There must be something else.

Postmodernism

Postmodernism tells us, in various ways, that we need to rethink our belief in science and progress itself. And it does more than this: postmodernism asks us some disconcertingly simple questions:

What, actually, drives human beings? Is it reason? Or is it not, in fact, desire, wishes, dreams, hopes, nightmares?

Rethinking our world

It is at this point that modernism takes us into the shopping mall, the movie theatre, the world of the child, including Disneyland itself.

Here's what one writer, Julia Cameron, says about movies. (Julia Cameron is an independent filmmaker and screenplay writer.)

> The movie camera takes us into all the odd, dark corners of our world and says, "You see? This is what's *really* happening".
>
> (Julia Cameron, in *The Artist's Way*)

The movie camera, then, may be a more reliable guide to reality and to what people are "really like" than any scientific or psychological journal. For it is the film world that explores the human story, human life. It is the film world that has examined, in all its horror, human violence and our worst nightmares. This violence and these nightmares, when they appear in scientific journals, come across as weak, unconvincing. Are clinical psychologists who interview serial killers in a maximum-security prison really going to begin understanding what leads to such deeds? Does a one-hundred-page report on such deeds and crimes really "speak" to us?

The movie camera has no such "scientific objectivity". It is prepared to show us just what happens during gang rape (*Straw Dogs, A Touch of Evil*), gang torture and killing (*Scarface, The Godfather*), racial hatred (*Mississippi Burning*). It will show us urban poverty (*Menace II Society*) and classroom violence (*Classroom 187*).

The movie camera asks us a question: Where do our shadow selves come from?

Question

Do you go to the movies? Have you ever seen a film containing explicit violence? What effect did this film have on you?

When faced with violence, scientific reason, by its very nature, cannot help us.

But science is guilty of more than simply failing to keep its promises. Science kills our dreams – either by examining them or by ignoring them. Read what one leading postmodernist, Jean-François Lyotard, says about his own dreams:

> Sometimes I dream that I am an astronaut. I land my spaceship on a distant planet. When I tell the children on that planet that on earth school is compulsory and that we have homework every evening, they split their sides laughing. And so I decide to stay with them for a long, long time ... well anyway ... until the summer holidays.

Where in the world are we going?

On the first day back at school in September David, aged seven and a half, comes home with the following homework: he has to learn this little story by Erhardt Dietl. In the space of one hour he can recite it in the right tone of voice without any mistakes. He has drawn the distant planet in his exercise book and the spaceship approaching it. The first thing that school makes him learn is the happiness of a world without school, with no obligations and no homework. The world exists only on another planet. It is reached in a spaceship. It seems just as natural as climbing on a bicycle. Years ago my sister and I would go off with two or three little friends, on long bicycle rides into the blue Atlantic summer, with our parents' blessing and our day's supplies of food on the carriers.

To educate is to lead out. The moderns have stressed the efforts necessary to lead and let oneself be led out of nature toward language. But "out" is possibly not "outside". It is no doubt within, far inside. One cannot reach it by uprooting oneself but by plunging deep within toward what is most intimate, where lies desire. The child knows a lot more than we do about the state of dependency not only in relation to adults, but to what he cherishes in itself, with or against "big people", well or badly.

When are we educated? When we know more or less which is the far-off planet we desire, and when we do all that we can to set off for it. If adults are often tough and sad, it is because they are disappointed. They do not listen well enough to the invitation to grace which is in them. They let the spaceship rust.

Adults take their holidays on the Riviera or in Florida. They really need them for their work exhausts them. To carry out their work, they have to give up their desire. Yet giving it up is impossible. In each of us there is an unconquerable resistance to the serious "ends" that social life proposes, a profession, a career, success. These ends count for nothing against a bicycle ride to another planet. This does not mean that I am advocating spontaneity as a pedagogical method and I don't believe that children are angelic. We are indebted to them and there is only one way to clear this debt, by assisting them to take off in their spaceship to the planet of their dreams.

(Jean-François Lyotard, in *Spaceship*)

Like Lyotard, who doesn't dream of a carefree world of summer picnics and no duties?

A group of people who are dreaming of such a world today are numbers of American schoolchildren whose parents voted for "stricter academic programs". In this programme, even kindergarten children of under six bring home homework.

Question

Does life really have to be about grim, stern duty?

Let's go back to the cinema again. If the cinema shows us nightmares, it also shows us dreams, hopes, illusions, beauty and fantasy. In an extraordinary and unforeseen way, the cinema mirrors our imagination. Who can forget Disney's *Fantasia*? Or the scenic beauty and queer sadness of *A River runs Through it*? Or the sense of overwhelming joy and loss in *The Lover*? Or even the more artificial splendour and excitement of the sweep of New York's huge buildings during the opening scene of *Working Girl*? Under the influence of such images, people have altered their lives, become dissatisfied with the "grim, stern duty" of life. Some have changed jobs, started extra-marital affairs or, faced with the relentless greyness of their lives, committed suicide.

Just supposing ...

Just suppose you were asked to direct or produce a film ...

Question

What would your film be about? Do you think it would be a happy film or a sad film?

Postmodernism also takes us into the shopping mall, a place where increasing numbers of people shop, socialise, eat ice cream. Many shopping malls today incorporate artificial scenery such as man-made lakes, small "forests", aquariums, bird houses. The shops and department stores that pay such high rents in these places know they are selling far more than merchandise – like the cinema, they, too, are selling images and dreams. Indeed, in the West, people increasingly define and see themselves in terms of "where they shop". Even basic, necessary consumables such as food itself are often sold in terms of image ("freshness", "healthy", "luxury imported chocolate", "good for your family").

Far from dismissing such claims as advertising grimmicks, postmodernism believes that human beings are deeply influenced by such claims. This is because we all naturally make associations and emotional connections with images. In short, we get a kick out of them. Such kicks may be trivial and silly, but – and this is where postmodernism is unique, perhaps postmodernism insists that silly, trivial "kicks" tell us something about what it means to be a human being.

Philosophers at work

Postmodernism does not believe in definitions and, in fact, a number of postmodern philosophers have even resisted being labelled "postmodern". Postmodernism examines the following aspects of the human condition:
- the way in which we see ourselves
- the failure of science to solve many problems
- the fact that reason may not be a good guide to solving certain problems
- the power of large, modern institutions over the individual (eg schools, hospitals, large business organisations)
- the need to experience all our emotions to the full, including our anger and sexuality
- our inner needs
- mental anguish and mental illness
- where we get our standards of right and wrong
- whether we can trust these standards
- criminality and delinquency (why are some crimes punishable and others not?)
- who defines what it means to be "a normal human being"
- whether technology is morally neutral.

Methods of enquiry in philosophy that have a connection with postmodernism:
- phenomenology (because phenomenology asks: Who are we?)
- hermeneutics (because hermeneutics believes symbols and images speak to us)
- empiricism (because empiricism asks: What is actually going on? Foucault claimed to be an empiricist)
- some forms of feminism (because feminism asks: Who says the male is the "norm"?).

People associated with postmodernism:
- Jacques Derrida
- Michel Foucault
- Jean Baudrillard
- Jacques Lacan

A good introductory book on postmodernism is *Postmodernism for Beginners* by R Applignanesi.

Postmodern writers

There are many writers of postmodern literature, and among the philosophers most are French.

Jacques Derrida – who died in 2004, focused on our need for deep relationships and our need for love and acceptance. He believed that modern political institutions such as the United Nations rely too much on legalistic political morality to bring about peace and solve problems. Derrida claimed that our "real enemy" is the person or act of "bad faith", in other words, any betrayal of trust.

Michel Foucault – died of Aids in 1984 and is probably the most famous of all postmodernists. He himself was traumatised by the demands of the French education system. His own innate homosexuality made him feel "abnormal" for much of his life. Being abnormal, Foucault asked a simple question: "Where do we get our beliefs about normality anyway? He came to the conclusion that such beliefs were inculcated into us by modern institutions (eg schools) who monitor us endlessly. It was Foucault who reminded us that the modern school is based on Prussian military ideals of punctuality, discipline, neatness, submissiveness to authority. Foucault's best-known book is *Discipline and Punish*.

Jean Baudrillard – focused on the power of imagery in the modern world and made a point of touring America and familiarising himself with American society. His book, *Simulacra and Simulation,* even discusses the influence of Disneyland on present-day human beings. Baudrillard was particularly interested in consumerism and what made people buy things. He also looked at how our sexuality was tied up in imagery and consumerism. It is sobering to know, then, that Baudrillard concluded that, in the end, human society is now in a deeply alienated state. His lasting impression of Disneyland itself was the feeling of "being abandoned" rather than enchanted.

Jacques Lacan – was, by training, a psychologist. But he came to reject many of the simplistic assumptions of Freud and believed that psychology needed to reject its early theories and be more humble in its claim to know "what made people tick". Lacan believed that human beings, like animals, are driven by basic needs: hunger, sex, need for contact with others. But, because of the enormous complexity of human social life, including human family life, as young children and even babies, we have to engage in various sophisticated communication patterns to have these needs met. In the process of doing so, we lose contact with certain parts of our psyche. Lacan had a long-standing affair with a well-known French movie actress and this too led him to focus on the question "Who are we?" in all its complexity.

Where in the world are we going?

Activity

Read the following excerpt. It is taken from Julia Cameron's book *The Artist's Way*.

> In order to thrive as people, we need to be available to the universal flow. When we put a stopper on our capacity for joy by declining the small gifts of life, we turn aside the larger gifts as well. Those of us who have stopped the flow completely will find ourselves in lives that feel barren and devoid of interest no matter how many meaningless things we fill them with.
>
> What gives us true joy? That is the question we need to ask. For each of us the answer is very different. For my friend Berenice, the answer is raspberries, fresh raspberries. She laughs at how easily pleased she is … For my friend Alan, music is the answer. Alan was a musician when he was younger, but he long denied himself the rights to play … Now he is working on his recovery, Alan allows himself the right to buy a new CD every week, a CD that sounds like fun. He's begun exploring. Gospel, country and western, Indian drum music … now he's finally gotten around to buying himself a drum set …

Raspberries, music. What do you think you might be denying yourself?

Does it work?

What postmodernism can help us to do

1. Re-assess the quality of our lives.
2. Resist pressures to turn into workaholics.
3. Gain more creative energy.
4. Question the claims of rigid morality.
5. Lead freer lives.

Where postmodernism fails

1. It may encourage destructive behaviour such as drug dependency.
2. It has not yet given us any alternatives to science as a way forward.
3. It underestimates the need for disciplined effort in any human endeavour.
4. It can lead to despair.
5. It is elitist. It needs to simplify its language to make it more accessible to non-intellectuals.

One man's life – Friedrich Nietzsche

Possibly one of the greatest ironies and tragedies was the neglect of the philosophy of Friedrich Nietzsche during the 20th century, a century that was blinded by scientific dogmatism, ideology (such as Marxism and the rise of religious fundamentalism), corrupt politicians and continual warfare.

Friedrich Nietzsche, possibly the first postmodernist, lived from 1844 to 1900. His father was a strict Christian pastor, but Nietzsche lost faith in Christianity while he was a student. A brilliant scholar and thinker, Nietzsche was a professor of philology (linguistics) when he was only 24.

Some of Nietzsche's works are:
- *Beyond Good and Evil*
- *Thus spake Zarathustra*
- *The Twilight of the Idols*
- *The anti-Christ*
- *The Gay Science*
- *Ecce Homo*

All these works contain the sacred, strange magic we referred to earlier. Sparkling, edgy, brilliant, bizarre and deeply disturbing, they wrestle continually with the question, "What does it mean to live fully as a human being?" None of these works are systematic. None of them are dull. They contain passages of poetical prose that rival Shakespeare.

> A drop of dew? An odour and scent of eternity? Do you not hear it? Do you not smell it? My world has just become perfect, midnight is also noonday, pain is also joy, a curse is also a blessing, the night is also a sun – be gone, or you will learn: a wise man is also a fool.
>
> Did you ever say Yes to one joy? O my friends, then you said Yes to all woe as well. All things are chained and entwined together, all things are in love; if you ever wanted one moment twice, if ever you said: "You please me, happiness, instant, moment!", then you wanted everything to return! You wanted everything anew, everything eternal, everything chained, entwined together, everything in love, oh that is how you loved the world …
> (From *Thus spake Zarathustra*)

The next piece is from *The Gay Science*:

> I derive a melancholy happiness from living in the midst of this confusion of streets, needs, voices: how much enjoyment, impatience, desire, how much thirsty life and drunkenness of life comes to the light of day every moment! And yet for all these noisy, living, life-thirsty people it will soon be so still and silent! How behind each of them stands his shadow, his dark companion! And all and everyone believes that what has been is nothing or little, this immediate future is all: and thus this haste, this clamour, this self-deafening, this self-overreaching!

Perhaps Nietzsche is telling us how he feels about shopping malls.

Nietzsche's life was a mixture of depth, tragedy, passion and, finally, madness. It is clear from his books that he was a passionate, almost ferocious man who believed that, whether we like it or not, our life, to be authentic, must be one of strife with the world about us and with the world within us. He himself was seriously unwell for most of his life, suffering from acute insomnia and attacks of migraine that left him temporarily blind. In 1889, when he was 45, he had a mental collapse from which he never recovered. For the rest of his life, he was cared for by his sister, Elizabeth. As far as we can tell, his intellectual abilities shrank to the equivalent of a six-year-old child. He once came upon his sister weeping and gently asked her: "Elizabeth, why are you crying? Are we not happy together?" A wounded healer, indeed.

The well-known composer Richard Strauss composed a symphony which he called *Also sprach Zarathustra*. He said the following about this music:

> I did not intend to write philosophical music. I meant to convey by means of music an idea of the development of the human race from its origin, through the various phases of its development, religious and scientific ...

Stanley Kubrick used this music for his film *2001: a Space Odyssey*.

Postmodernism in a nutshell

Postmodernism is a response to the bewildering world of technology and virtual reality that has mushroomed over the past twenty years or so.

Postmodernism is a Western philosophy but, ironically, since it takes seriously the human condition *in whatever form that takes*, it can engage in dialogue with African philosophy.

If we ignore postmodernism, then we are, in fact, ignoring what our world is. People who ignore postmodernism tend to be rather closed people with rigid value systems they are not prepared to question. Such people can be faced with sudden catastrophe and find themselves ill-prepared to cope.

Rethinking postmodernism

It has been some six years since we wrote the pages you have just read, on postmodernism.

In those six years, one of the authors of this book has been rethinking postmodernism: To what extent is postmodernism a passing, intellectual fashion that bears little relation to "real" philosophy or "real" intellectual endeavour? Of course, we know that this is to beg the question: Who defines "real" philosophy and intellectual endeavour from something that is bogus?

We accept this criticism, but there are certain things about a great deal of postmodernist writing that are disquieting.

- A large proportion of postmodernist writing *is* obscure to the point of meaninglessness, and some thinkers, particularly the British empiricist Richard Dawkins, have derided postmodernism as little more than a hoax. Dawkins may be overstating the case, but we certainly think that postmodernism will have to start speaking more clearly if it is to be any use in the ordinary world.
- Even if we accept that some postmodernist writers are trying to express complex and profound thinking, we query whether their academic jargon is the best vehicle for expressing this profundity. Perhaps we *should* just "go to the movies" for this sort of thing. Or read literature. Or do art.
- Postmodern philosophy is notoriously difficult and time-consuming to understand. If it does not help human beings solve "real-life" problems, what is the point of it?
- Postmodernism itself claims to be "not serious". In a world threatened by religious terrorism and political fanaticism, perhaps we need serious philosophies that can deal with these forms of unreason.
- We have said that "science kills the soul", and that "science was not keeping its promises". The view that science necessarily encourages a grey and drab approach to life is, we think, now suspect. In fact, science is about exploration. And there is no reason to regard science as the enemy of either art or poetry. It is, however, the enemy of traditional forms of institutionalised religion.
- One postmodern philosopher, whose writings are easier to read, is Michael Foucault. It is important to remember that Foucault specifically claimed to be an empiricist.

Perhaps a good place to end this section on is to quote the empiricist Steven Pinker, who works in the field of neuroscience and psychology:

> Maybe philosophical problems are hard not because they are divine or irreducible or meaningless or workaday science, but because the mind of *Homo sapiens* lacks the cognitive equipment to solve them. We are organisms, not angels, and our minds are organs, not pipelines to the truth.
>
> (from How the Mind Works)

Conclusion

At the very beginning of this book, we said:

> Philosophy is the asking of difficult and subversive questions.

Now, at the end of this book, we could rephrase this statement:

> Philosophy is the asking of simple and subversive questions.

These are simple questions about what is right or wrong – about whether it is possible to find out what is right or wrong. These are simple questions about why people are unhappy – simple questions about how we are living our lives, about whether life is worth living. These are simple questions about truth and falsity.

What happens if we never ask these questions, Ii we ignore philosophy completely? Can we live like this?

The answer, we believe, is "yes". We can indeed go through life without knowing anything at all about philosophy, about the leading figures in philosophy, about the various forms of philosophy. We do not have to question why we live as we do and we certainly do not have to question why the world is the way it is.

But if we do this – that is, if we ignore philosophy – then we are putting ourselves at risk. We will be vulnerable to society's "power ploys", to manipulation, to false promises, to fanatical ideologies.

Philosophy, far from being an "ivory-tower" activity, makes us "streetwise". It sharpens our mental abilities, makes us alert, makes us alive, empowers us to act, enables us to "sniff out" falsity and duplicity. For these reasons alone, philosophy needs to be taken seriously.

The world today is facing huge problems. Ecologists tell us that we may have only a few decades, if that, before the planet itself starts to suffer irreversible damage and, eventually, is unable to support human life. If they are correct, if we are killing this planet, then we need to ask how and why and we need to be wary of plausible, "easy" answers.

Environmental damage is only one crisis. War, conflict, misery and suffering seem to be part of our lot as human beings. Can we do anything about this? It may be that we cannot. It may be that suffering is an intrinsic part of human life.

But the greatest danger is that, without the tools of philosophy, we may make this suffering worse, not better. We may be tempted to listen too willingly and too eagerly to people who claim to have answers. These people are likely to be leaders of cult religions or people selling some sort of new ideology. Or they may control organisations such as the United Nations or the World Bank. All of them are likely to wear the mask of goodness.

Only philosophy can help us be on our guard against this type of falsity.

Only philosophy can help us confront the world, confront ourselves, rethink the world, rethink ourselves. This is the invitation contained in the pages of this book.

Bibliography

APPIAH, K A. 1992. *In My Father's House: Africa in the philosophy of culture.* New York: Oxford University Press.
APPLIGNANESI, R. 1995. *Postmodernism for Beginners.* Cambridge: Icon.
BEHRENS, G. 1999. Over the Rainbow. *Time,* 7 June: 30.
BROTHER THOMAS. 1987. *The Path to the Beautiful.* Boston: Godine.
CAMERON, J. 1992. *The Artist's Way.* New York: Tarcher.
CARVER, R. 1989. *A New Path to the Waterfall.* New York: Atlanta.
CASSON, L. 1966. *Ancient Egypt.* Aylesbury: Time-Life.
COETZEE, P H (ed). 1998. *Philosophy from Africa: a text with readings.* Johannesburg: Thomson.
DUNBAR, R. 1995. *The Trouble with Science.* London: Faber & Faber.
FIENNES, R. 1975. *Where Soldiers Fear to Tread.* London: New English Library.
FILLINGHAM, L J. 1994. *Foucault for Beginners.* London: Writers & Readers.
FRENCH, M. 1988. Reissue edition. *The Women's Room.* Out of print.
FRIEDAN, B. 1963. *The Feminine Mystique.* Harmondsworth: Penguin.
FULGHUM, R. 1988. *All I really need to know I learned in kindergarten.* New York: Villard.
GORDON, L R. 1997. *Existence in Black: An Anthology of Black Existential Philosophy.* London: Routledge.
GORE, T. 1999. Drop the Stigma. *Time,* 10 May: 52.
HILLMAN, J. 1966. *The Soul's Code.* New York: Random.
HOLLINGDALE, R J. 1987. *A Nietzsche Reader.* Harmondsworth: Penguin.
HOUNTONDJI, P. 1983. *African Philosophy: myth and reality.* Indiana: Indiana University Press.
JUNG, C. 1964. *Man and his Symbols.* London: Picador.
JUNG, C. 1986. *Selected Writings,* with an introduction by A Storr. London: Fontana.
KING, N Q. 1986. *African Cosmos.* Belmont, California: Wadsworth.
KING, S. 1986. *It.* London: Hodder & Stoughton.
KNAUER, K. 1996. *Great People of the 20th Century.* New York: Time Books.
KOKA, K. 1998. *What is African Philosophy: concept and application.* Johannesburg: Goethe Institute.
KRUGER, J S. 1995. *Along Edges. Religion in South Africa: Bushman, Christian, Buddhist.* Pretoria: University of South Africa.
KUNDERA, M. 1984. *The Unbearable Lightness of Being.* New York: Harper & Row.
LEAKEY, R & LEWIN, R. 1992. *Origins Reconsidered: in search of what makes us human.* London: Little Brown.
MARX, K & ENGELS, F. 1848. *Communist Party Manifesto.*
MARX, K. 1942. *Das Kapital.* London: Dent.
MICKELL, G. 1997. *African Feminism: the politics of survival in sub-Saharan Africa.* Philadelphia: Philadelphia University Press.

MUTWA, C. 1996. *Isilwane: the animal.* Cape Town: Struik.
NIETZSCHE, F. 1986 [1883]. *Thus spake Zarathustra.* Harmondsworth: Penguin.
NIETZSCHE, F. 1987 [1885]. *Beyond Good and Evil.* Harmondsworth: Penguin.
NIETZSCHE, F. 1987 [1886]. *Ecce Homo.* Harmondsworth: Penguin.
NIETZSCHE, F. 1987 [1888]. *Twilight of the Idols/The Anti-Christ.* Harmondsworth: Penguin.
O'ROURKE, P J. 1998. *Eat the Rich.* London: Picador.
OGUNDIPE-LESLIE, M. 1994. *Re-creating Ourselves: African women and critical transformation.* New Jersey: Africa World Press.
OKEKE, P E. 1996. Postmodern Feminism and Knowledge Production: the African context. *Africa Today,* vol 3 (1).
ORBACH, S. 1991. Reissue edition. *Fat is a Feminist Issue.* Out of print.
PETERS, M. (ed) 1995. *Education and the postmodern condition.* Westport, Connecticut: Bergin & Garvey.
ROBINSON, S. 1999. Out of the Abyss. *Time,* 7 June: 23-27.
SACKS, O. 1995. *An Anthropologist on Mars.* London: Picador.
SCHAEF, A. 1992. *Women's Reality: an emerging female system in a white male society.* San Francisco, California: Harper.
SPENCER, L & KRAUZE, A (eds). 1996. *Hegel for Beginners.* Cambridge: Icon.
STORR, A (ed). 1986. *Jung: selected writings.* London: Fontana.
TEFFO, L J. 1994. *The Concept of "ubuntu" as a Cohesive Moral Value.* Pretoria: Ubuntu School of Philosophy.
WILBER, K. 2001. *A Brief History of Everything.* Dublin: Gateway.
WIREDU, K. *Philosophy and African culture.* Cambridge: Cambridge University Press.
WOLF, N. 1990. *The Beauty Myth.* London: Chatto & Windus.

Acknowledgements

CARVER R. Iowa Summer. © Raymond Carver to 1988; 1989 to 2006, copyright by Tess Gallagher.
    for quote on p. 38
DAVISON, M. 1954. *A handweaver's pattern book.*
    for pattern on p 121
DIACK, J MICHAEL. s.a. *The laggard left.* London: Paterson's Publications Ltd.
    for music notation on p 120
DIKENI, S. Afrikan Workers Lullaby. p 37
D'SOUZA, D. 2002. For article on p 55
KRUGER, J S. 1995. *Along edges.* Pretoria: University of South Africa.
    for photographs on p 122
MALAN, R. 1998. *The Essential Steve Biko.* David Philip & Mayibuye Books: Cape Town.
    for quote on page 129
O'ROURKE, P J. Extract from *Eat the Rich* on page 63
THE HOLY BIBLE. 1973. Nashville, Tennessee: Dove Bible Publishers, Inc.
    for print on p 5 (Jesus Christ)

Recommended reading

Chapter one

Ayer, A J. 1971. *Language, truth and logic.* Revised edition. London: Penguin.

Websites

http://en.wikipedia.org/wiki/Logic
www.mtnmath.com/whath/node20.html
www.owenbarfield.com
www.iep.utm.edu/w/wittgens.htm

Chapter two

Epstein, R L. 2002 *Critical Thinking.* Belmont, California: Wadsworth.
Randi, J. 1989 *The Faith Healers.* Buffalo, NY: Prometheus.
Sogolo, G. 1993 *Foundations of African Philosophy: a definitive analysis of conceptual issues in African thought.* Ibaban: Ibaban University Press.

Websites

http://www.austhink.org/critical/
www.skeptic.com

Chapter three

Bediako, K. 1995 *Christianity in Africa: the Renewal of a non-Western Religion.* Maryknoll, NY: Orbis.
Lewis, R G. 1997 *Existence in Black: An Anthology of Black Existential Philosophy.* London: Routledge.
Martel, Y. 2001 *Life of Pi.* Edinburgh: Canongate.
Masolo, D A. 1994 *African Philosophy in Search of Identity.* Bloomington, ID: Edinburgh University Press.

Chapter four

Higgs, P., Vakalisa N C G, Mda, T V, Assie-Lumumba, N T. 2000. *African voices in education.* Cape Town: Juta.

Chapter five

Wilber, K. 2000. *Brief history of everything.* Boston: Shambala.

Chapter six

African feminism

Amadiume, I. 1997 *Re-inventing Africa: matriarchy, religion and culture.* New York: Zed

Dolphyne, F A. 1991 *The Emancipation of Women: an African perspective.* Accra: Ghana University Press

Obioma, N. 1998 *Sisterhood, Feminisms and Power: from Africa to the Diaspora.* Eritrea. Africa World Press

Obioma, N. (ed). 1994. *The politics of (M)othering: womanhood, identity and resistance in African literature.* London: Routledge

Ogundipe-Leslie, M. 1994 *Re-creating Ourselves: African women and critical transformation.* New Jersey: Africa World Press

Feminism theology

Harvey, A. 1996 *The Divine Feminine: exploring the feminine face of God throughout the world.* Berkeley, California: Conari Press

Harvey, A. 1998 *Son of Man: the mystical path to Christ.* Tarcher/Putnam

Feminism

Brennan, S. 2003 *Feminist Moral Philosophy.* Calgary: University of Calgary Press

Friedan, B. 1963 *The Feminine Mystique.* Harmondsworth, Penguin.

Somerville J. 2000 *Feminism and the Family.* New York: Macmillan

Tuana N. and Tong R. 1995 *Feminism and Philosophy.* Boulder, Colorado: Westview Press

Chapter seven

Wilber, K. 1985. *No boundary: Eastern and Western approaches to personal growth.* Boston: Shambala.

Chapter eight

Jung, C. 1979. *Man and his symbols.* London: Aldus Books.

> This is the classic western text on symbolism. However, symbolism and imagery are probably the most culture specific of all human experiences. Even our interpretation of colour is influenced by our culture. In western society, the colour red symbolises danger – in some eastern cultures, however, it represents spiritual strength and power.

> So, rather than go to a book we recommend, we suggest you think about symbolism in your own culture, community and life. Has any particular symbolism or imagery helped you in a difficult situation? Do you carry a religious symbol on your person or, say, in your car?

Chapter nine

Wilber, K. 1998. *The marriage of sense and soul.* New York: Random House.

Index

A
Achiever (Type Eight Personality) 69
affirmative action policy 82
affluence, western 57
African feminism 88, 90–91
African philosophy 44–55
  and feminism 99
African traditional thought 46
Allah 111
American feminism 88, 91–97
Amin, Samir 55
analysing statements 7
Ancient Egyptians 112–113
anthropology 116
Appiah, Kwame Anthony 46, 47
Arendt, Hannah 23
argument
  false 27–30
  logical symbolism and 11–12
asking questions 17–31
assumptions, hidden 7–9
Atwood, Margaret 99
Ayer A J 10

B
Baudrillard, Jean 34, 128, 135
beating the system 71–102
Bergman, Ingmar 108
Biko, Steve 45, 129
Bishop Tutu 69
Black Consciousness 45
black existentialism 41
Bodunrin, Peter 46, 47
British feminism 88, 91–97
British school of philosophy 16
Buddha, Gautama 71, 72–73, 109, 111
Buddhism, 103–104
Buddhist mandala 119
Bushman rock art 121–122

C
Cabral, Amilcar 46, 47, 71
Cameron, Julia 132, 137
capitalism 57, 63–65
Carver, Raymond 38–39, 105–106
Castro, Fidel 63
Chinweizu 55
Christianity 44–45, 111
colonialism 55–59
colour symbols 119–120
Communism 74
Constitution, South African 1–2
consumerism 128
cosmic phenomenology 107
critical rationalism 30, 46
  and feminism 96, 99
critical theory 71–102
  and feminism 96, 99
cultural identity and Ancient Egyptians 112–113

D
Dalai Lama 33, 107, 113
Daly, Mary 97, 99
darkness, symbol 126–127
Dawkins, Richard 109–110, 140
De Beauvoir, Simone 34
deconstruction 82
democracy 57, 81
Derrida, Jacques 34, 81–82, 86, 107, 135, 136
Dikeni, Sandile 37–38
D'Souza, Dinash 55
Du Bois W E B 34

E
Egyptians, Ancient 112–113
Einstein, Albert 23, 107, 114, 117–118
emotion, appealing to 29
empiricism 13–15, 46
  and critical rationalism 23
  and feminism 96, 99
  and postmodernism 135
Engels, Friedrich 74
enneagram 65–69
ethnic philosophy 45
European feminism 88
existentialism 34–42, 46
  and hermeneutics 123
  black 41

F
fact 12–13
fallacy of the *ad hominem* argument 28
false arguments 27–30
false cause-and-effect 28

falsely representing an opinion 28
falsity 107
Fanon, Frantz 34, 46, 47, 55, 56
feminism 71, 88–102
    African 88, 90–91
    and postmodernism 135
    British and American 88, 91–97
    European 88
    first-wave 88, 96–97
    Islamic 88, 97
    second-wave 88
feminist theology 97–98
first-wave feminisim 88, 96–97
Foucault, Michel 34, 35, 39, 71, 76–78, 86, 135, 136, 140
French, Marilyn 99
Friedan Betty 99
Freire, Paul 71
Fulghum, Robert 24, 86
fundamentalism, patriarchal 97

G
Gbadegesin, Segun 47, 54
gender politics 90
God 8
Gordon, Lewis R 41
Grameen Bank 100–101
Greer, Germaine 99
Gyekye, Kwame 47, 107

H
Habermas, Jürgen 71
Hawking, Stephen 23, 117
Hegel, Georg 127
Heidegger, Martin 107
Helper (Type Two Personality) 66
hermeneutics, 116–129
    and postmodernism 135

hidden assumptions 7–9
Hillman, James 33, 108
holon 83–84
Hountondji, Paulin 46, 47
human existence, mystery of 107–108
humanism
    ubuntu 47
    Zambian 45
human rights 3–4

I
Ichazo, Oscar 65
ideal child 77
identity 110–111
individual pretence 107
Individualist (Type Four Personality) 67
inner reflection 104
Irigaray, Luce 34
Islamic feminism 88, 97
Islamic fundamentalism 97

J
Jesus of Nazareth 67, 71, 72, 73–74, 111
John Paul II, Pope 67
Jung, Carl 124–125

K
Kandinsky, Wassily 118–120
Kaunda, Kenneth 45
King, Martin Luther 107
King, Stephen 126
Koka, Kgalushi 34, 53
Kundera Milan 80–81
Kunstler, James, Howard 49

L
Lacan, Jacques 135, 136
language 116
    philosophy and 6–7
Leakey, Richard 54, 114, 116
life, meaning of 32–42
light, symbol 126–127

linguistic analysis 9–11
linguistic meaning 10
logic 10
logical empiricism 16, 30
    and feminism 99
logical symbolism 11–12
Loyal Supporter (Type Six Personality) 68
Lyotard, Jean-Francois 132–133

M
mandala 119–120
Mandela, Nelson 23, 66
Marx, Karl 71, 72, 74–75
Marxism 71
mathematical symbolism 117–118
Mbiti, John 47
meaning
    of life 32–42
    of symbols 123
    of words 3–7
    Wilber 128–129
Middle Way 111
Mill, John Stuart 96
Millett, Kate 99
model child 77
modernism 130–131
Mohammed 71, 73, 109, 111
morals 24–27
Moses 71, 72, 73
Moses the Black 45
Mott, Lucretia 91–92, 95
Mother Theresa 66
movie camera 132
Movie Star (Type Three Personality) 66–67
multilevel marketing (MLM) 30–31
Mutwa, Credo 84–85, 107

N
name calling 28
Nandy, Ashis 55

Index

Nazism 71
Negritude 45
New York Stock Exchange 64
Ngugi Wa Thiong'o 47
Nietzsche, Friedrich 34, 37, 67, 138–139
nihilism 39
Nineteenth Amendment, USA 96
Nkrumah, Kwame 45, 46
normalisation 78
Nyerere, Julius 45, 46

O

objectivity and morals 24
Okolo Chuwudum 107
open-mindedness 22
opinion, falsely representing 28
oppression of women 94–95
O'Rourke, P J 63–64
Oruka, Henry Odera 46, 47
Oshita, Oshita 107

P

patriarchal fundamentalism 97
patriarchy 90
Peacemaker (Type Nine Personality) 69
personality system (enneagram) 65–69
phenomenology 103–115
  and postmodernism 135
  and science 109
philosophy
  African 44–55
  and language 6–7
  ethnic 45
  pure 46
  sage 45–46
Picasso, Pablo 67
Pinker, Steven 109–110, 140

Plato 7
Pleasure-seeker (Type Seven Personality) 68
political philosophy 46
Polkinghorne, John 9
Pope John Paul II 67
Popper, Karl 23
popular view and truth 29
postmodernism 71, 130–141
power
  creating 80–81
  shape of 75–78
Project Independence 100–101
pure philosophy 46
Pythagoras 65

Q

qualia 110
questions, asking 17–31

R

real world 106–107
reflection 104
Rerformer (Type One Personality) 66
religious leaders and social criticism 72–75
Rodney, Walter 55
Russell, Bertrand 10

S

sage philosophy 45–46
Said, Edward 55
San rock art 121–122
Sartre, Jean-Paul 34
science
  and phenomenology 109
  and western affluence 57
scientific rationalism 22
scientific socialism 45
scientific thinking 18–24
Scientist (Type Five Personality) 67–68
second-wave feminism 88

self, phenomenology of 106
Senghor, Leopold 45, 46, 47
senses, experience gained through 12–13
Serequeberhan, Tsenay 47
shopping mall 128, 134, 139
signs, Baudrillard and 128
social criticism, religious leaders and 72–75
social falsity 107
socialism 71
social phenomenology 107
Socrates 22
Sogolo, Godwin 23
Sojourner Truth 96
South African Constitution 1–2
Soyinka, Wole 55
Spivak, Gayatri 55
Stanton, Elizabeth Cady 91–92, 95
statements
  analysis of 7
  of fact 12–13
  truth of 9–11
St Augustine 44, 111
St John of the Cross 109
subjective consciousness 110
Sufism 111
Suzman, Helen 23
symbolism
  colour and 119–120
  mathematical 117–118
  musical 120
  San rock art 121
  weaving 121
symbols, universal 117–128
  Jung 124–125
system, the 61
  beating 71–102
systems theory 61–102
  and ourselves 65–69

T

Teffo, Joe 47
theory of everything 83
Touré, Seko 45
Trotsky, Leon 71
truth
   and morals 24
   basic structure of 12
   of statements 9–11
Tutankhamen 86
Tutu, Bishop 69

U

ubuntu 47–48, 66
ujamaa 45

V

values and critical
   rationalism 24–27
verifiable facts 10
violence 132
von Bertalanffy, Ludwig 64

W

weaving symbols 121
western affluence 57
Wilber, Ken 9, 82–84, 128–129
Wiredu, Kwasi 46, 47
wisdom, philosophy of 45–46
Wittgenstein, Ludwig 10
Wolf, Naomi 99
Wollstonecraft, Mary 95
women, oppression of 94–95
women's movement *see* feminism
women's rights 95–96
words, meaning of 3–7

Y

Yunus, Muhammad 100–101

Z

Zambian humanism 45